I0822923

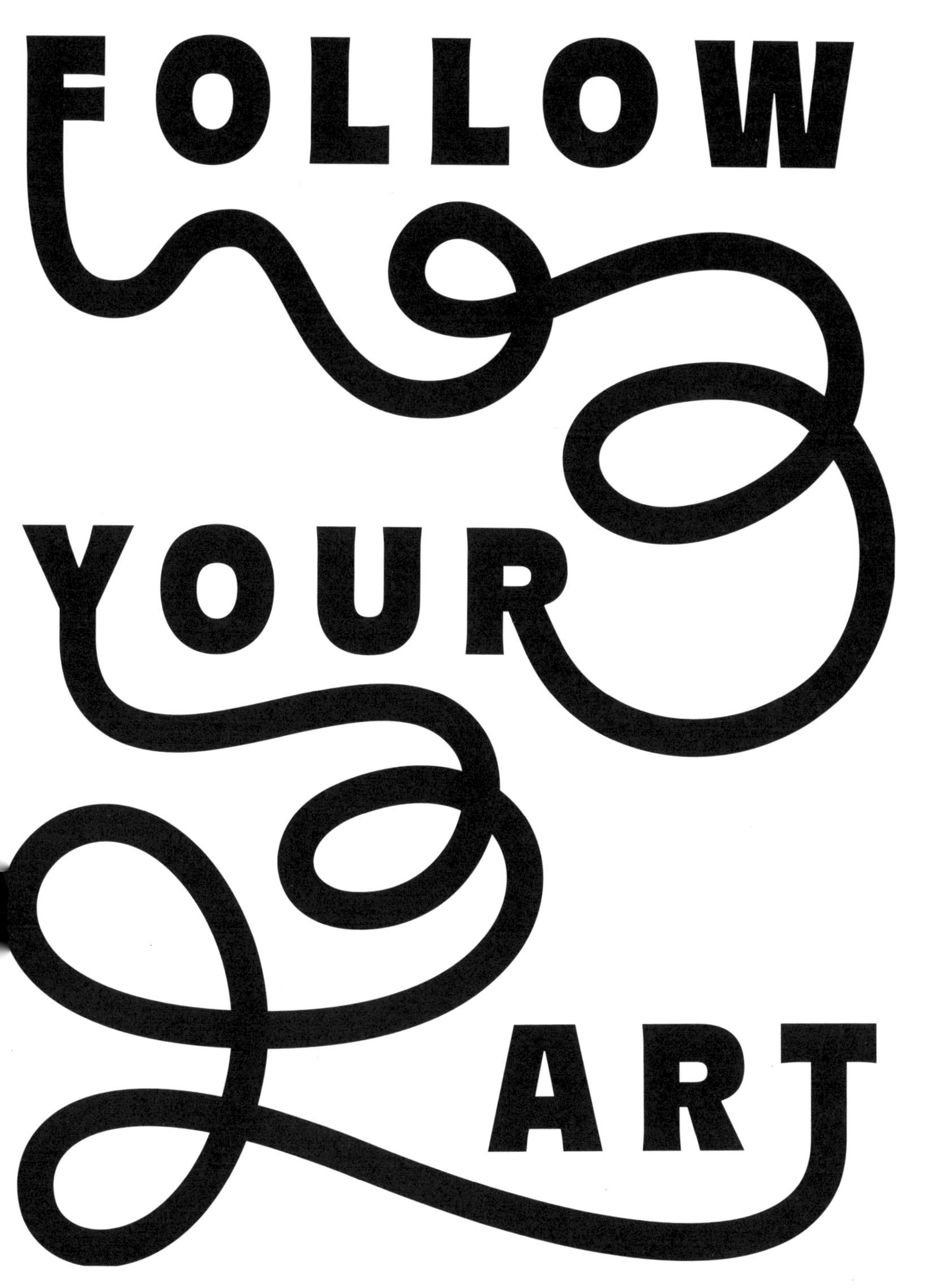
FOLLOW
YOUR
ART

Editor: Soyolmaa Lkhagvadorj
Designer: Jenice Kim
Managing Editor: Lisa Silverman
Production Manager: Larry Pekarek

Library of Congress Control Number: 2025941435

ISBN: 978-1-4197-7682-3
eISBN: 979-8-88707-400-9

Printed and bound in China
10 9 8 7 6 5 4 3 2 1

Abrams books are available at special discounts when purchased in quantity for premiums and promotions as well as fundraising or educational use. Special editions can also be created to specification. For details, contact specialsales@abramsbooks.com or the address below.

ABRAMS is represented in the UK and Europe by Abrams & Chronicle Books, 1 West Smithfield, London EC1A 9JU and Média-Participations, 57 rue Gaston Tessier, 75166 Paris, France.
www.abramsandchronicle.co.uk and
www.media-participations.com
info@abramsandchronicle.co.uk

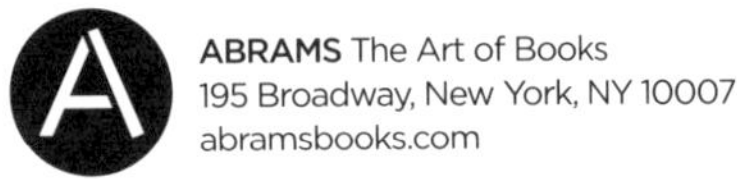

FOLLOW YOUR ART

Uncover & Unleash Your Creative Voice

Katie Johnson
& Ilana Griffo

Abrams, New York

CONTENTS

INTRODUCTION

Your Secret Sauce

This is a book about being an artist. But, more importantly, it's a book about being yourself.

As a creative person, you've inevitably had to face the infamous "blank canvas" and all of the giant question marks that follow. "What should I make?" is simultaneously every artist's favorite and least favorite thought. It's somehow equal parts exhilarating and scare-your-pants-off intimidating.

> ***When everything is possible . . . where do you even start?***

In this book, we'll help you answer that question for yourself. Spoiler alert—it all begins with getting to know who you really are, aka uncovering your creative identity. But before we get into all that, we've got to talk a bit about sauce.

In Mexico City, there's a famous restaurant, consistently named one of the best in the world, called Pujol. Pujol is helmed by chef Enrique Olvera and is perhaps best known for one dish in particular—the Mole Madre.

(That's mole as in "moe-lay," a thick, delicious sauce that's often served at Mexican holidays and celebrations—not an unwelcome growth or a little burrowing mammal.) As with a typical mole, the Mole Madre is made of a very long list of ingredients. Lots of chilis, tomatoes, spices, nuts, and chocolate all harmonize together to make a deep and complex flavor profile that tastes like nothing else you've ever tried before.

It takes patience and love to make a good mole; it's not something to be rushed. You need to roast and char and ground and sauté. And most importantly, you need to give it time to develop, something the Mole Madre does better than any other mole. Pujol's famous sauce has literally had thousands of days to evolve and mature. Every time it gets close to running out, the chefs simply add a new batch to the original mixture. There's a little blank line on the menu next to the Mole Madre so that at each dinner service, someone can handwrite the number of days that the sauce has been . . . *alive?* We're not sure if that's a little gross or just totally cool, but no matter what it is, people seem to agree that it tastes *freaking delicious.*

The thing is, the Mole Madre doesn't taste like any one of its ingredients. It tastes like *all of them,* and then some. Every component works together to make this really special, unique flavor that's truly greater than the sum of its parts. It's so interesting that you eventually stop searching for what's in it and just resign yourself to enjoying it.

> ***That's what you are. You're a big, hearty bowl of Mole Madre.***

Your influences and experiences are the ingredients. Everyone who has come into your life, every TV show you've binged, every trip you've taken, every success or failure, every time someone has treated you with kindness or made you laugh—all those things go into the pot and bubble and boil and intertwine to make something absolutely original. You can't taste any of the individual parts, but the result is something that's unique and exciting and wholly *yours*.

As time goes on, your complexity only grows. With each new iteration—every season of change—you add a new, fresh batch of experiences and perspectives to the old ones. You can expand and build on the you that was there before. It can get richer and deeper, but you'll never be without at least some trace of the original.

In the following chapters, we're going to help you get in touch with your unique mole recipe. You'll get to know exactly which ingredients go in and what delicious flavors result. Then, we'll figure out how all of that applies to how you present yourself as an artist. In other words, we're gonna look deep into that bowl and figure out the recipe for your particular brand of *special sauce*.

To uncover the components that make you who you are, we'll start by asking you questions and guiding you through introspective exercises. Then, you'll see how those traits and qualities manifest within your art as we dive into a series of fun, creative experiments. Finally, we'll help you identify the visual and conceptual hallmarks of your creative identity that emerge and show you how to express that identity to others with clarity and confidence. You'll learn how to talk about yourself as an artist in a way that feels authentic to you and makes people excited to hire you, buy from you, and become your true fans.

This is going to be an awesome adventure, and we couldn't be happier that you're here to take it with us. So go ahead and put on an apron, friend, 'cause we're about to get cookin'.

CHAPTER 1

Plotting the Course

Who Are We (and Why Are We Here?)

Now that we've reeled you in with way more sauce talk than you ever expected from a book about art, it's probably about time to tell you who we are and why we give a hoot about finding your artistic identity in the first place.

The first thing you should know is that there are two of us: Ilana and Katie. We're self-employed artists, business partners, and friends who met via an Instagram DM, and we actually live across the country from each other. We're perpetually thankful to the World Wide Web for bringing us together and allowing us to work our dream jobs from New York and Texas while in our pajamas.

Before we ever knew each other, we had very similar paths and experiences as artists. We both studied graphic design in college and went on to accept jobs as art directors afterward. However, despite landing the roles we thought we wanted, we eventually realized that something was missing. We weren't feeling fulfilled, and we just didn't see ourselves continuing our career paths at design or advertising agencies and climbing the corporate ladder. The thought of leaving that trajectory behind was scary, because we'd been taught that working at agencies was the only route to "success" as an artist. No one had really presented other options to us, and we certainly didn't know anything about running our own art businesses.

So, naturally, that's what we decided to do. We each made the incredibly nerve-racking decision to leap into self-employment. Ilana made the jump after she landed a single gig that would eventually and unexpectedly pay more than her full-time job (holy cow!), and Katie put in her notice after making a forty-page business plan that detailed every step she planned to take after leaving. We both decided to focus on hand lettering as our primary art form, and we began building product lines, selling stationery, greeting cards, planners, art prints, etc., while also taking freelance projects on the side.

We were ravenously consuming any and all resources on creative entrepreneurship that we could find but were quickly frustrated by the general lack of information around our specific type of businesses. There was so much we had to figure out on our own, and it was really difficult to find other folks who were dealing with the same things we were. Over the years we tried a lot of different strategies, sold all sorts of different products and services, failed a lot, girlbossed too close to the sun at times, and worked our butts off. Eventually, we began to find our footing and *finally* started to feel like the real business owners we'd previously only "pretended" to be. (Don't be fooled though, we're still making it up as we go a lot of the time.)

Around 2018, Katie posted about an online course she was working on to teach other artists about art licensing, a lesser-known income stream that she'd begun to tap into by designing products like greeting cards for other companies to sell. Ilana saw the post and sent Katie a message to say that she'd been thinking of creating a course on the same topic. After initially feeling discouraged that someone else had the same idea (the nerve!), Katie decided to suck it up, shift her mindset, and ask Ilana if she'd be open to collaborating on the class.

And that's how we teamed up to create our first course: Art Licensing for Letterers. We learned several important, eventually life-changing things in the process. (We also learned how to correctly spell it after embarrassingly getting called out in the comments of our announcement post for "Art 'Liscensing' for Letterers." How cringey is that?!) Most importantly, we realized we work really, really well together. Finding each other was like finding the yin to our yang. Ilana excels at making quick decisions and taking immediate action, while Katie brings deep, strategic thinking and attention to detail. It was such a great match from the get-go that we knew we had to hold on to each other.

Because of our similar backgrounds and experiences building our own businesses, we also found ourselves on the same page with our visions for the future. We'd both become increasingly passionate about making business education more accessible for artists.

> ***We wanted to help remove the roadblocks keeping other creatives from building the careers and businesses they deserve to have.***

So, when we were on the phone one day mulling over ideas about how to expand our educational resources beyond our course, Katie ushered in the next phase of our partnership with one fateful yet woefully anticlimactic phrase: "I guess we're starting a business together."

We called ourselves Loomier, a nonsense name that we invented in hopes that it would be easier to trademark. But alas, we came to rue the day we chose it, as everyone was rightfully confused and constantly mispronouncing it. Thankfully, the name Loomier was put to rest after only about a year when we, incredibly, got the opportunity to take over another business that we'd known and loved for many years: Goodtype.

Goodtype initially began in July 2014 as an Instagram account by founder Bode Robinson. It rapidly gained traction for sharing, you guessed it, good typography from artists around the world. In fact, the reason Ilana was following Katie in the first place before sending that initial direct message was because she'd seen Katie's work featured on Goodtype.

In January 2021, in a very full-circle moment, we became the new co-owners of the account that had meant so much to us. We dove in headfirst, careful to keep the culture of sharing inspiration and gorgeous type intact while also adding the component of education that we'd become so passionate about. Since we took the reins, we've created many more courses, hosted countless workshops, started a conference and a podcast, and have done everything we can to help artists tackle the intimidating world of entrepreneurship.

Through all these touchpoints over the years, we've worked with a *lot* of artists and students, and it's actually because of them that we're here writing this book today. We've been in the trenches with creatives in all stages of their careers, helping them navigate their frustrations and hang-ups along the way. And, since we're artists too, we've gone through all the same stuff (even as we're writing

the road to excellence begins unimpressively

STEPHEN
GUISE

this book). We know intimately where support is needed and which struggles tend to come up most. And the number-one topic that drives artists completely nuts—the question we see over and over in our comments, workshops, coaching sessions, and email inbox—is *"How do I find my style?"*

Because we've had to respond to this question so many times, and because we've had to work through it ourselves, we've spent a lot of time thinking about it. It's a big topic that requires a big answer, and we're really excited to delve deeper and give it the proper explanation it deserves. However, deciding on the kind of art you want to make and how you want to make it requires more than just reading someone else's ideas—it requires getting really introspective about your own. We'll give you as much guidance as we can, but a huge part of the process of finding yourself is *taking action*.

That's why we're going to ask you to make art—to draw, experiment, try different mediums, and see what bizarre, wonderful, amazing things you can unlock inside your brain. These exercises are designed to help you find a new perspective when you're feeling stuck (a feeling we know well!) and to help you see your work holistically instead of looking for answers in a single piece of art in a vacuum. You'll unearth ideas you didn't know you had in you, and you'll learn a lot about yourself in the process. We'll be searching for patterns and throughlines in the artistic choices you make throughout the activities so we can better understand the qualities that make you unique. And then we'll connect all the dots to understand what all of it means and how you can harness it.

If you thought you could put your feet up and speed-read this book, we're (not) sorry to say . . . you're about to get more bang for your buck than you'd anticipated! If you really want to get to know yourself as an artist and feel much more confident about what to create next time you encounter a blank canvas, you'll need to get your hands dirty.

But don't worry—while it *is* going to be a workout for your brain, we're gonna have *so much fun* along the way.

Why Your Creative Identity Matters

We've already explained that your creative identity is complex, layered, and constantly evolving—just like Pujol's Mole Madre. We talked about how all your experiences and interactions blend together to shape your understanding of the world and influence the things you choose to create. But we haven't yet addressed why any of that is meaningful. Why should we bother trying to understand ourselves? Why is having a clear creative identity so important for artists?

There are two sides of those questions to consider. First, why is it important for you, and second, why is it important for others? Let's talk about you first.

Being a human is chaotic. We've got a lot going on inside our heads (especially those of us who are neurodivergent). So many memories and emotions and thoughts are swirling around that it can be hard to get a grasp on them sometimes. We're incredibly complex, so much so that we often make decisions or take actions without fully understanding our motives, and that can lead to feeling out of sync with ourselves. But, when you take the time to really get in touch with your creative identity and who you are on a deep level, you can make decisions with much more confidence and ease. When you've got a grasp on your values, your core motivations, the things that you love or want to avoid, you can see the choices you want to make with so much more clarity! Instead of feeling overwhelmed by all the possibilities of a blank page, you'll have a much narrower vision of where to begin and where you ultimately want to go.

When you're dialed into your creative identity, it helps other people, too! You know how you can come across something in a store and immediately think, "Oh that's SO [insert friend's name here]"? We all know that person who's super easy to shop for because you can so clearly see their distinctive voice in everything they do. As artists, our goal should be to be that person. We want everyone—especially our potential fans and clients—to really understand the type of work we make, to remember it, and to be able to explain it concisely when they tell someone about it.

FROM KATIE

As someone who struggles with perfectionist tendencies, I find that the beginning of the design process is often the hardest part for me.

If I don't give myself constraints, I will spend far too much time considering every possible idea in hopes that eventually I'll find the "best" one. But, since there's no such thing as the "best" idea, I end up feeling paralyzed by all the options. Understanding the key components of my creative identity, like my love for details, helps me focus and make decisions more confidently. The more I understand about what I enjoy and where I really shine, the more clarity I have about how to start a new project!

Think about an art director who works at an ad agency. They get a new project for a client that requires an illustrator, and they start rifling through their mental filing cabinet of artists who might be a good fit to hire for the project. *You want to be in that filing cabinet! Preferably . . . right at the top!* When an art director chooses an artist for a job, it's because the story and voice behind their work is clear, compelling, and memorable (and it must also align with the needs of the project, of course). While that art director may have encountered plenty of people who could probably do the job well, they will only think to hire the ones whose portfolio made a distinct impression and had a unique point of view. Art directors also look for artists whose work is consistent. A consistent body of work gives the client an idea of what they can generally expect you to make, which gives them confidence enough to hire you. The more you weave cohesion and harmony throughout the art you share, the more you'll tick those boxes and start to find your way into those proverbial filing cabinets.

While we're talking about the importance of consistency, cohesion, and harmony in your work, we definitely need to take a moment to define exactly what we mean here, because this concept is a big, foundational part of this whole book. When some artists hear "cohesion," they may immediately think "restriction." You might assume, at first, that we're advising you to confine yourself to a singular style of art-making, like black and white charcoal drawings, for example. If the idea of *only* creating in charcoal for the rest of your days sounds like your particular brand of torture, don't fret, because that's definitely *not* what we're suggesting.

There's a big distinction between your creative *identity* and a *style*. The primary objective of this book is to help you discover your creative *identity*, which means understanding who you are as a whole, creative person. A style, as we see it, is one small subset of your overall creative identity. It's one approach to how you make art, and it's only one of many potential flavors in your metaphorical ice cream shop.

YOU CAN'T HELP BUT BE YOURSELF!

To come at this idea from another direction, imagine that your creative identity is like an entire language. It's your whole vocabulary—every word you've ever learned and have to draw from. Your style, on the other hand, is how you actually *communicate*—what you choose to say and how you say it. You may change the way you communicate and the words you use based on who you're talking to, how you're feeling, or as you're learning and changing throughout life. Similarly, artists can have multiple different styles and ways of expressing themselves. They might juggle several different styles at the same time, or styles may come and go over longer periods during their careers.

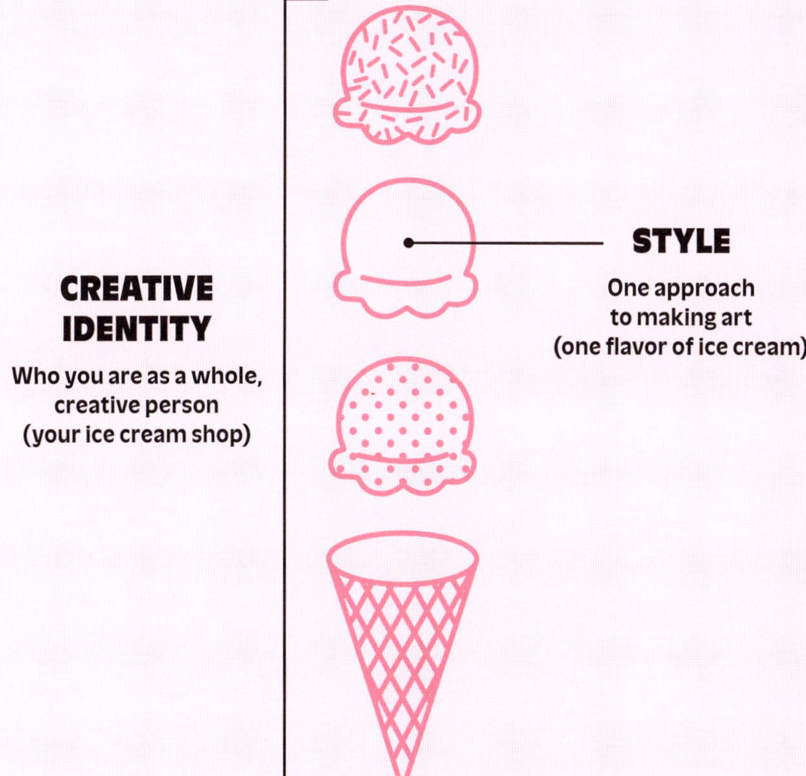

Even though you may explore different styles, mediums, collections, or niches (more on this later), there are *always* consistencies and threads that weave them all together under your unique stamp.

> ***You may not realize it yet, but your fingerprints are all over everything you create!***

Whether you're crafting a pot out of clay, designing a logo, or painting on a canvas, you'll always make choices that nobody else would make. Together, we'll begin to identify those consistencies that make your art *yours,* and we'll help you become even more intentional about how you incorporate them into your work moving forward.

Now, we know you have a *lot* more questions about all of this. How do we even begin to understand something as complex as our creative identity? How do we stand out from the crowd and the endless conveyor belt of content and inspiration online? How do we leave room for experimentation and play while also creating a cohesive body of work?

We can practically feel the questions piling up in your brain already. We'll get to them all, we promise! It's just about time to start delving into the "how" of it all. But, before we dive in headfirst, let's make sure we're going into this work with the right mindset and with clarity about what we want out of it in the end.

Now's the time to commit to actually completing the prompts and exercises in this book (alas, simply looking at them will not give you all the answers you're looking for via osmosis). This process will be fun, but you'll have to be vulnerable along the way, and you'll also need to *do the work* if you want to reap the rewards!

the beginning is the most important part of the work.

PLATO

MINDSET EXERCISE

There's a concept from Zen Buddhism called shoshin, which roughly translates to "beginner's mind." This idea encourages us to always approach life with the curiosity and humility of a beginner, focusing on the excitement that comes from infinite possibilities instead of believing we already have all the answers.

Take a few minutes to close your eyes, center yourself, and concentrate on adopting a beginner's mindset as you prepare to dig into this book.

Suggested Meditation:

This moment, like every moment, is fresh, new, and unrepeatable. You've never been here before. Yet, how often do we enter the present already filled with ideas, assumptions, and expectations? These thoughts weigh us down, keeping us from experiencing the world with the openness we deserve.

Take this time to release any need to prove yourself. Let go of the belief that you already know what will happen, how things work, or what others expect of you. Instead, focus on the boundless potential available when you approach life with a fresh, creative spirit. Like a beginner, see with new eyes, unencumbered by the past or predictions of the future.

Feel this mindset flow through you. Let it transform how you see, how you create, and how you approach the following pages.

SETTING INTENTIONS

Next, set some intentions and define what you're hoping to glean from this experience. When we clearly identify our questions, we're much more likely to find the answers.

What do I want to get out of this book?

What are my biggest questions or roadblocks when it comes to finding my creative identity that I would like to overcome?

CHAPTER 2

Getting to Know Yourself

We humans are like hungry little vacuum cleaners who never stop slurping up the endless external stimuli around us. We're constantly internalizing information and then remixing and distorting it, filtering it through our unique understanding of how the world works. Because everyone has different influences, backgrounds, and emotions through which they process information, every person ends up having a totally original experience of life. We're all completely distinct, and that's a beautiful thing!

The problem is that a lot of people lose sight of their uniqueness, or they see it as a roadblock instead of a superpower. If you want to be a better, more confident artist, the first step is to *actively look* for the qualities that make you different. Can you think of an artist you truly love who is simply blending in and doing what everyone else is doing? Probably not. Great artists aren't afraid to stand out and embrace the traits that set them apart. The more you see and understand yourself, the more others will see you and be able to connect with you, too.

Throughout the exercises in this chapter, you'll search for your own differentiators and begin to piece together the foundational building blocks that make you who you are. You'll work to identify the fundamental "ingredients" that make up your mole (or perhaps you see yourself more as a smoothie or a layer cake), as well as the common threads that run throughout your personality and preferences. It's important to note that we aren't asking you to *add* any ingredients to your recipe—we just want to uncover the existing components so you can amplify and celebrate them!

We've broken this chapter into several parts. In the first section, we'll take a look at your personality, the experiences and memories that have shaped you, and your interests outside of art. Then, we'll dig into your artistic inclinations by examining the sources of inspiration that speak to you most and uncovering what you like about them. Finally, we'll look at several artists who have clear and distinctive creative identities and figure out the underlying traits that give their work a consistent voice.

As we do this work, we want you to consider several things. First, keep your eyes open for connecting threads or consistencies that show up in your answers. Are there patterns that arise in how you think or approach life? Perhaps you're a deep thinker, and you'll discover that you need a complex, emotional connection to really appreciate a piece of art. Maybe you grew up in a mid-century modern–style house, and now you find yourself pulled toward vintage 1960s motifs that remind you of your childhood. Can you see a bigger story emerging as you respond to these prompts?

Sometimes, finding the throughline between our interests, tastes, and experiences can be tricky, but that doesn't mean it's not there. For example, someone who loves surrealist art, heavy metal music, and skydiving may see those interests as totally separate parts of themselves. But when we look closer, we can find that there's a pattern of appreciation for things that are adventurous, statement-making, and a little off-kilter. The truth is, we typically like lots of different things for lots of the same reasons.

> ***So, keep your eyes open for new connections that you may not have noticed before!***

Another thing we want you to remember is that finding yourself is an ongoing process. When we look at other artists who have a really strong, unique point of view, it might seem like it comes to them effortlessly. It's as if the divine art spirits have blessed them with the ultimate vision and sense of self, and that every creative endeavor they attempt turns to gold. But trust us, it doesn't work that way for anyone. There is always a *ton* of effort involved behind the stuff that looks easy. That artist you admire, whoever it is, has been through a freakin' *Frodo-goes-to-Mordor* kind of journey to get to the place they're at today. As artists, we all have to do a lot of self-examination and experimentation before we develop a real awareness and confidence in our creative identities. These prompts are a step in the right direction, but this won't be where the story ends (and that's the fun part!).

It's time to go deep into that extraordinary brain of yours, see what's rattling around inside, and figure out how it all fits together to make you the person you are! Grab a cup of whatever tasty drink floats your boat, get comfy, and let's get introspective.

DON'T WAIT

UNTIL YOU

KNOW WHO

YOU ARE

TO GET

STARTED

AUSTIN KLEO

WHO ARE YOU?

PERSONALITY

Our personality informs so much about the art we ultimately choose to make—from the emotions we aim to evoke in others, to the amount of time and energy we're willing to spend on a piece, to the environments we find most inspiring.

What do you know about yourself?

Write down as many words as you can that describe parts of your personality. Feel free to focus only on stuff you like about yourself, or consider things you'd like to change if you're up for it. If you get stuck, try thinking of traits that others regularly point out to you.

(for example: good listener, tidy, funny, energetic, detailed, etc.)

What traits do you admire in other people?

. . . .

What traits do you dislike in other people?

. . . .

What are your biggest fears? How might they affect your creative work?

. . . .

What are the three most important items in your home and why?

. . . .

What is a quote that resonates with you on a deep, soul level? Why?

. . . .

What would your ideal day look like (and who would you spend it with)?

. . . .

EXPERIENCES

Our life experiences shape the way we see the world around us. Understanding the impactful moments and relationships that made us who we are can help us make more authentic and meaningful creative work.

What childhood experiences do you remember having an impact on you? Describe how these events affected you long term.

What images stick out in your mind from childhood?

(for example: cartoon characters, cereal boxes, primary colors, your backyard, etc.)

What shows or movies were your favorites as a kid?

What words come to mind when you think of your childhood?

Which places hold the most meaning for you and why?

What's the best gift you've ever received and why?

When in life have you had the most fun?

When in life have you felt most afraid?

What's a memory you wish you could relive over and over? What emotions does it bring up?

When in life have you felt happiest?

TIMELINE:
Create your own timeline to represent the most important events and changes in your life, and think about what you've taken away from each "era."

OTHER INTERESTS

We're more than just the job title we hold. The more of ourselves we share with people, the more seen and understood we'll feel. Consider how your interests outside of art could overlap with or play a role in your creative output.

What hobbies do you enjoy now?

What kind of music do you like, and what qualities do your favorite musicians share?

What else do you do in your free time?

What are your all-time favorite TV shows or movies, and what do you like about them?

What topics outside of art really fascinate you?
(for example: quantum physics, politics, elephants . . . get nerdy with it!)

What career would you have had in another life?

What are your guilty pleasures?

What would you do in life if you weren't afraid?

What are you bad at?

WHAT DO YOU LIKE?

Turn the page to start creating your mood board!

We can learn a lot about ourselves by investigating our own personal tastes and asking questions about why we're drawn to certain characteristics or themes over others.

CREATE YOUR PERSONAL MOOD BOARD

Put together a collection of visuals that really speak to you. The goal is to create a compilation of things that "feel" like you.

✳ Where to source your images

You can hop over to Pinterest, take screenshots of inspirational images on your phone, or even print out pictures or cut them out of magazines.

✳ What to include

Consider adding pieces by your favorite artist, a color palette that makes your jaw drop, an outfit with a pattern so cool it gives you goose bumps, your dream living room, etc.

✳ Where to create it

You can create a virtual mood board (using a Pinterest board or a program like Canva or Adobe Express—whatever works for you!) or a physical mood board (by cutting and pasting images into the space provided on the following page). It's up to you which feels better and more fun to create!

✳ Keep in mind

Don't worry about things "matching" right now. Your board is going to be a mash-up of different influences. Once you've finished, take stock of any consistencies you're seeing, and then use your board to help you answer the follow-up questions on page 40.

MY PERSONAL MOODBOARD

List 5 to 7 words that describe the overall feeling of this mood board.

(for example: nostalgic, mysterious, humorous, delicate, loud, etc.)

Is there a particular style, trend, or period of art history that comes to the forefront in these images?

(for example: mid-century, art deco, Scandinavian, rustic, minimalist, industrial, etc.)

What colors are you most drawn to?

(for example: neutrals, neon color pops, black with an accent color, pastels, etc.)

What subject matter do you gravitate toward?

(for example: portraits, florals, still life, spaces, etc.)

What kind of shapes do you see?

(for example: simplified geometric, realistic, organic, lots of circles, etc.)

What textures are represented?

(for example: gritty, smooth and flat, natural brush textures, spray paint, etc.)

Additional notes and insights:

FROM ILANA

When doing these exercises for myself, I didn't really have a big, revolutionary "a-ha" moment.

I did, however, notice some smaller trends that helped me get a better understanding of myself, like how much I crave structure and organization. These seemingly unimportant realizations gave me so much more insight and direction than I expected as I sat with them. I know you'd love your very own "a-ha" moment where the clouds clear and the birds sing, but give it a little time. It's amazing how these little discoveries can add up and snowball into your creative work in ways you never imagined when you just give them a chance.

Decoding Creative Identity

Now that you've identified some of the building blocks of your own creative identity, the next step is to figure out how all those ingredients can work together to tell the full story of who you are as an artist.

First, let's look at a few examples of how other artists combine their own building blocks into a distinctive, recognizable identity that spans across all their work. We'll pay close attention to how they utilize different elements of style, such as color, texture, and shape, to convey their own stories. Check out the Elements of Art Glossary on page 43 for the full list of terms you can consider when decoding other artists' identities—or your own!

WHEN YOU BASE *your* *work* ON WHAT YOU *care* ABOUT YOU'LL HAVE *work* THAT SAYS *something*

ESO TOLSON

THE ELEMENTS OF ART GLOSSARY

It's much easier to evaluate a piece of art when we break it down into smaller pieces. The following terms will help you consider the many different qualities that work together to create the whole. It is by no means a complete list, but it's a great starting point that you can use throughout this book and in your life.

Color:
What colors are used? Are they muted or saturated? Warm or cool?

Texture:
Is there texture in the work? What kind of textures, if any, do you see?

Shape:
Are the shapes soft or hard? What shapes are repeated? Are they realistic or abstract?

Perspective:
Is there dimension and depth or is the work flat? Do we see the subject head-on, or are we viewing from the side or even above?

Line Work:
What do the lines look like? Are they delicate or thick? Is there an outline around the graphics? Are the lines all one weight, or do they change in size throughout?

Rhythm and Movement:
Is there repetition? Does the placement of lines, shapes, or colors purposefully lead the eye around the piece?

Composition:
Is the layout vertical or horizontal? Is it zoomed in on a subject or far away? Is there a lot of negative space, or is there rarely a break for the eye?

Hierarchy:
What objects are largest and which are smallest? Where does your eye go first?

Subject Matter:
What is the theme or subject of the work? What is the piece saying to us from a conceptual standpoint?

Who Is William Morris?

William Morris was a British textile designer, often referred to as a founder of the Arts and Crafts Movement. Despite having created a whopping number of patterns and designs, his voice resonates consistently throughout every piece. His work can be found in galleries and museums worldwide, and although most of it was created in the late 1800s, it can still be found today in stores like Williams-Sonoma, Anthropologie, and H&M.

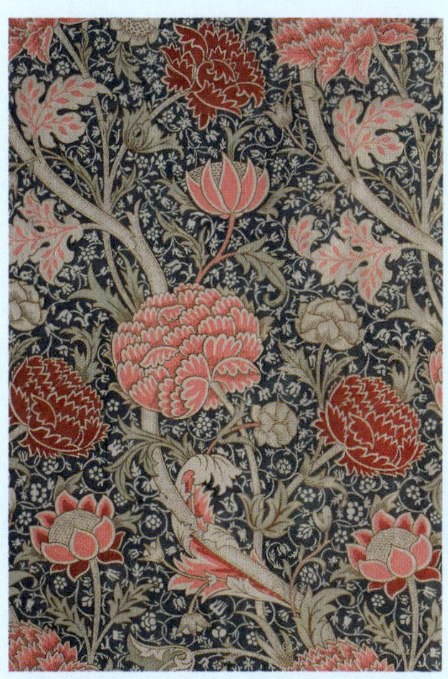

Color:

Morris gravitates toward rich, lush, organic tones. His colors have an earthy quality, although sometimes he dials up the saturation for a more dramatic impact. You'll see an abundance of shades of greens and hues that would be found in nature.

Texture:

As a textile designer in the 1800s, Morris created many of his prints using a block printing method. The carving process used in this technique creates its own texture that adds dimension and depth to his work. Craftsmanship was very important to him, and imprints from the tools used in his production process remind us of the artist's hand behind each piece.

Shape:

Organic shapes are immediately recognizable as natural elements but are often exaggerated to enhance their beauty. These enhancements add to the feeling of luxury and elegance that flows through Morris's work.

Line Work:

Intricate lines are used to add shading and meticulous detail. Objects are also outlined, making them feel fantastical and idealized instead of overly realistic.

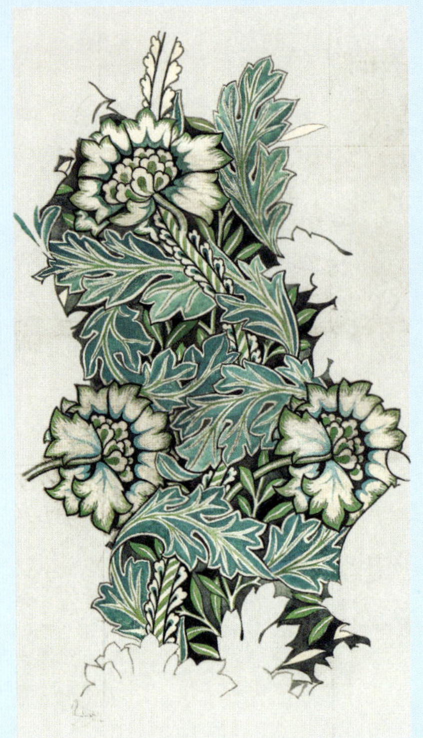

Subject Matter:
Much of Morris's work highlights the beauty of nature, featuring gorgeous botanicals and bird motifs. As a social activist, Morris aimed to bridge the gap between classes, believing that beauty is something everyone should be able to enjoy—a philosophy he infused into his work.

Morris's Artist Statement (as We'd Imagine It):
William Morris's desire to replace the questionable production standards of factories with careful craftsmanship by individuals dictated much of what he ultimately created. We can see an outpouring of care and dedication to quality in the meticulous details that appear in every piece he made. The textures and imprints left from handmade production methods also remind us of his intimate involvement through every step of the process. His commitment to bringing beauty into the homes of ordinary people, not just the elite, is clear in the way he elevated and exaggerated natural flora into luxurious patterns for wallpapers and textiles that could adorn their homes.

The Takeaway:
We love that there's a clear story that flows through Morris's work. There are personal beliefs that underlie his choices as an artist, and his visual aesthetic is simply a natural extension of who he is as a person.

While your story almost certainly won't be the same as Morris's, we hope it'll get your wheels turning about *your* bigger picture, and how your beliefs and personality traits might ultimately lay a foundation for the artist you'll become.

The true secret

of happiness

lies in taking a

genuine interest

in all the details

of daily life

William Morris

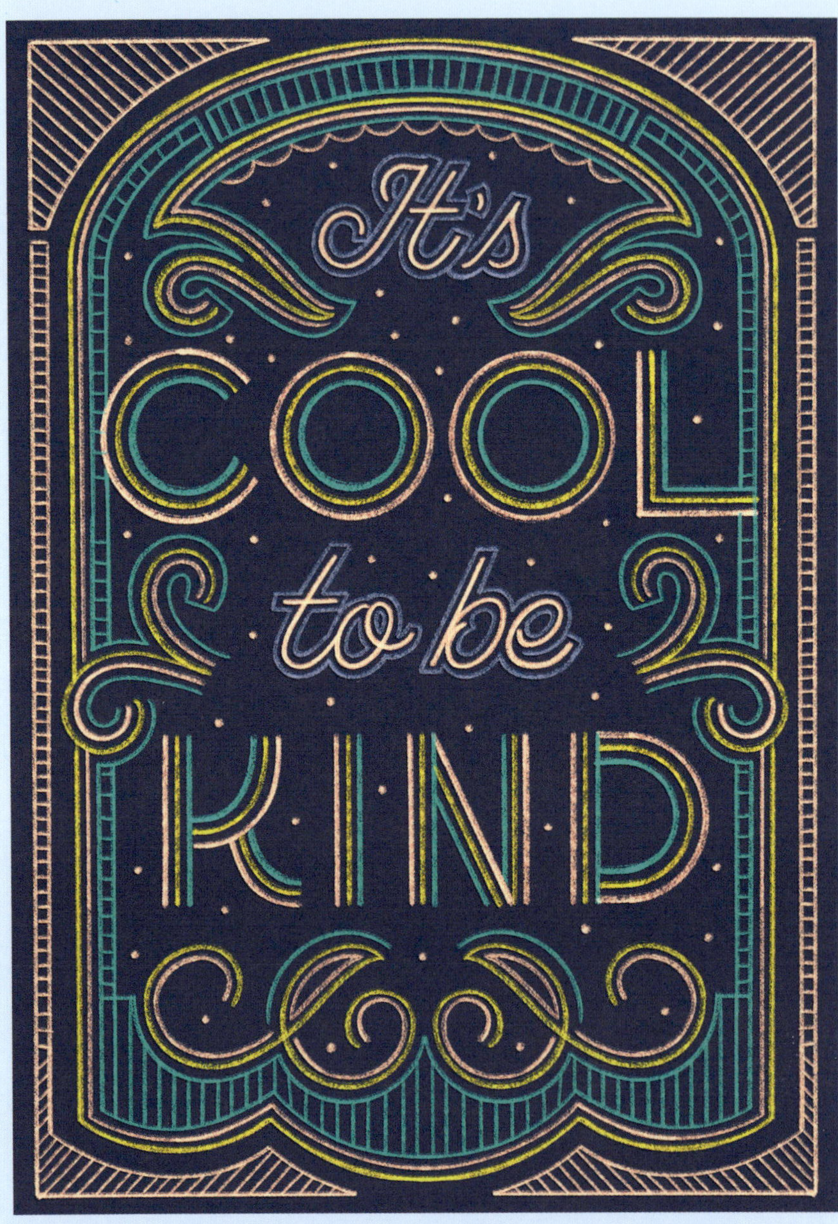
It's
COOL
to be
KIND

Who Is Katie Johnson?

Other than being the co-author of this book and co-owner of Goodtype, Katie is a graphic designer, lettering artist, and musician. She's just as likely to be found watching her favorite reality TV show as she is to be tucked in a dark corner, deeply entrenched in work. Katie can concentrate on one tiny detail for longer than anyone ever should, but she can also be fun and lighthearted. She's a curious person who is a deep, strategic thinker, but she's also not afraid to crack a joke. Katie really values authentic connections with people and is always trying to lean into the funny, relatable moments that level the playing field and remind us all we're not so different at the end of the day.

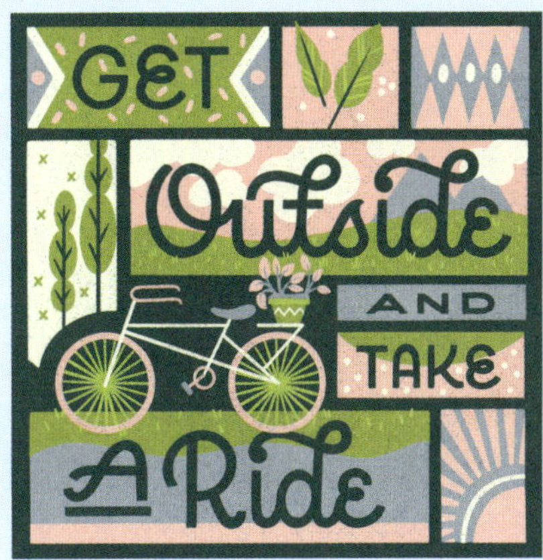

Color:

While Katie likes to experiment with color, she gravitates toward soft combinations and muted pastels. She's a glutton for pinks but is careful to use them in strategic amounts so they don't turn a cute moment into a Pepto-Bismol nightmare.

Texture:

Katie's work features tons of tiny details. Even if she leaves some negative space, it's likely that she'll add some texture in there so nobody's bored. She incorporates her favorite grainy textures in almost every piece to add dimension, but tries to dial them back so they never become a distraction.

Shape:

Katie's art nouveau influences are clear in her obsession with ornament and love for flowy, organic shapes.

Line Work:

Katie frequently uses lines and dots as details to add motion and interest throughout her work.

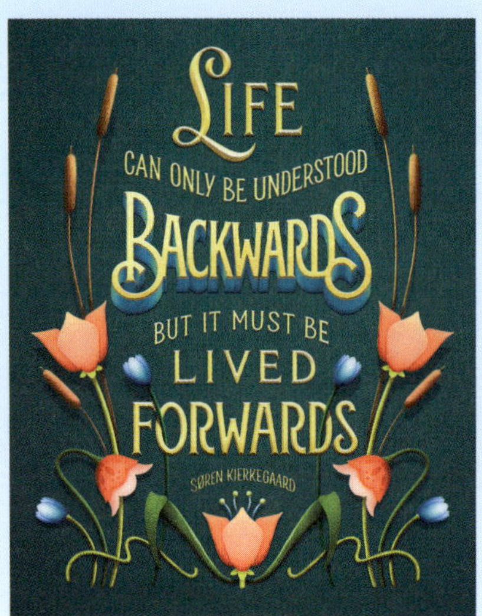

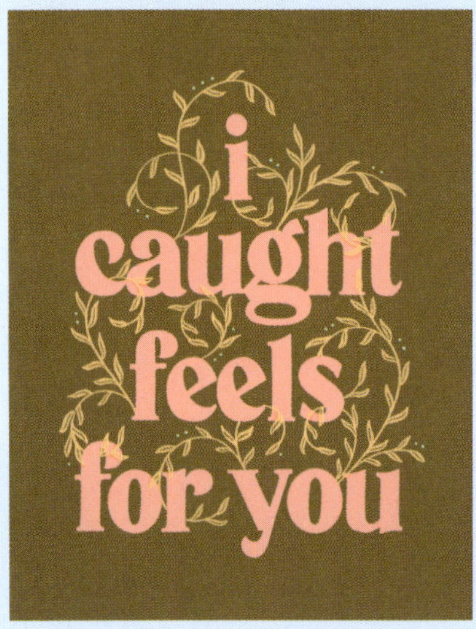

Subject Matter:
Because of her strength in copywriting, Katie's work focuses on words. Her language is playful, personable, and often funny, while its artistic execution is usually polished and ornate.

Katie's Artist Statement:
Katie's work is easy to spot because it perfectly balances precision and play. From a saucy greeting card to a strategically placed flourish, her voice oscillates between polished and lighthearted, and often mixes the two. Her creations tend to feature an art nouveau influence, which comes out in curving lines, ample decorations and ornaments, and dynamic compositions. When her color choices and crisp lettering pair with her witty charm, we get something beautiful but also very relatable and human.

The Takeaway:
Katie's duality is what makes her unique. She embraces the complexity of who she is—both careful and considered *and* lighthearted and playful—and the combination is both relatable and memorable.

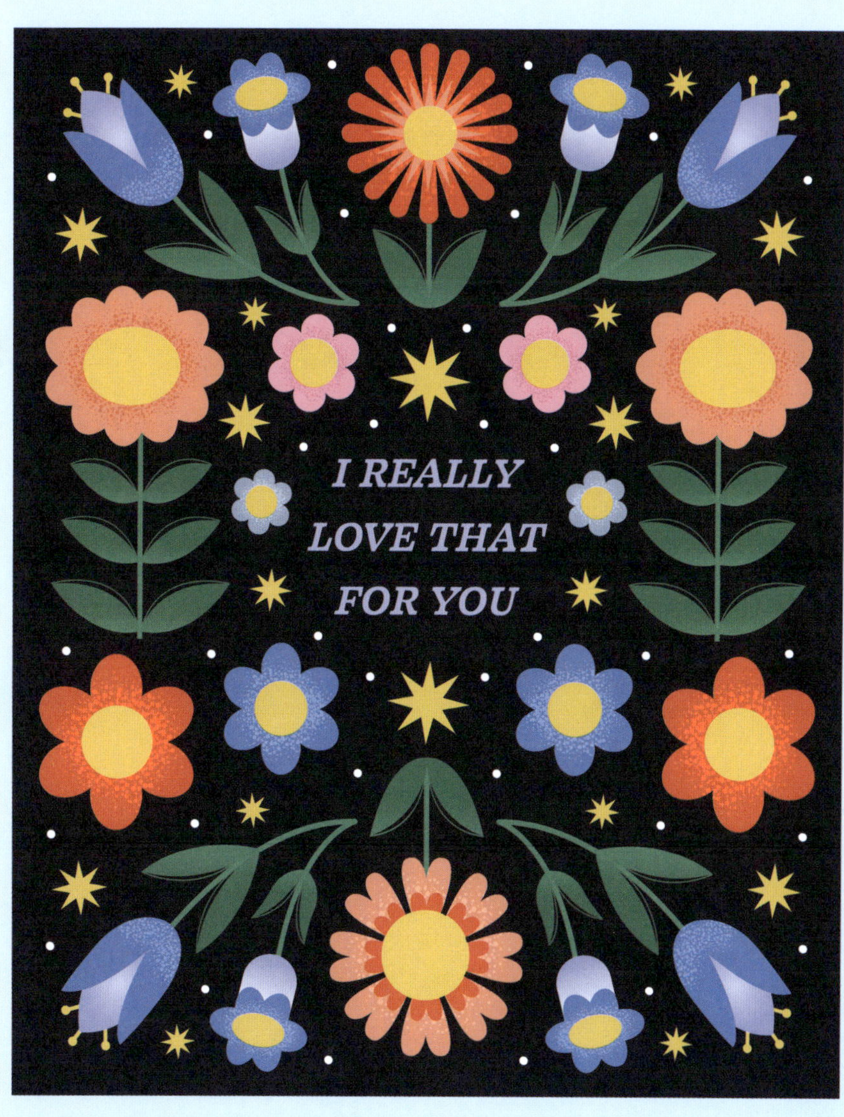
I REALLY
LOVE THAT
FOR YOU

Who Is Ilana Griffo?

On top of being co-author of this book and co-owner of Goodtype, Ilana Griffo wears many hats. She is a graphic designer, lettering artist, author, and mother. She's a quick-acting go-getter, and her superpower is taking matters into her own hands and making her own dreams come true! She's brave, always upping the ante for herself, and has a natural ability to connect with people. Ilana's always willing to help out, whether she's teaching a course, giving a pep talk to a friend, or showing up with flowers at your doorstep when you're feeling down.

Color:

Ilana's personal work features vibrant pops of color, rarely without the support of her favorite duo, black and white.

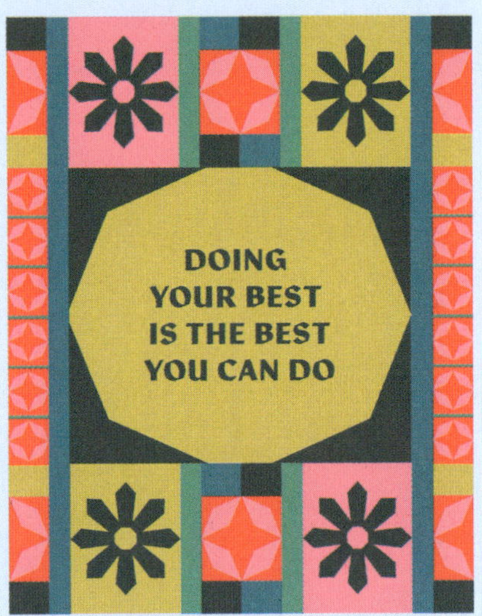

Texture:

Ilana's work is light on texture, often utilizing a simple grain to add visual interest or imply dimension. Her work is clean and fresh and tends to be pretty flat and graphic.

Shape:

In keeping with her approachable aesthetic, Ilana uses shapes that are based in geometry but are intentionally imperfect. From a wonky checkerboard pattern to a slightly lopsided flower, Ilana reminds people that quirks are what make them special.

Line Work:

Ilana uses simple, rudimentary lines and dots to add subtle accents throughout her work.

Subject Matter:

Ilana's work is uplifting and inspiring, often featuring hand-drawn messages with cheerful supporting graphics. She's not interested in drawing things realistically, but rather in signaling, through an intentionally simplified aesthetic, that her art is a safe space.

Ilana's Artist Statement:
Ilana infuses her warm personality into her work, capturing a vibe that just feels *good* from the messaging to the aesthetic. Her work gives us all the pep talk we need and wraps us in a big, warm hug. As someone with ADHD (attention deficit hyperactivity disorder), Ilana rides the line between minimalism and maximalism, finding clarity in constraints. Aesthetic imperfections and purposefully simplified shapes welcome us into Ilana's unpretentious world and help us feel comfortable there. Her work strikes a balance between timeless and on-trend that never feels fussy or overdone, and in the end, reminds us of what really matters.

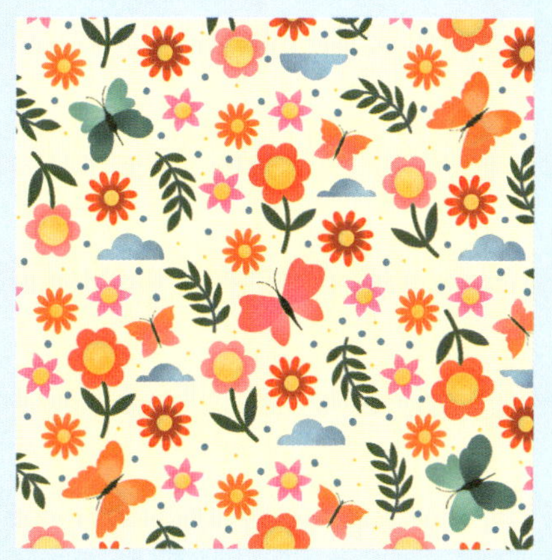

The Takeaway:
Ilana's art expresses her personality and underlying drive to help people feel better and more like themselves. By making approachable, unpretentious work, she gives people an instant signal that they're invited into her space.

Next Steps

We've just spent a lot of time delving deep into the traits that make other artists unique, as well as collecting inspirational images and analyzing them in your mood board. Learning from artists we admire, finding inspiration, and distilling our influences are a huge part of the process of discovering your own identity. But it's also important to make sure the art that comes out of all that exciting inspiration is fully authentic to you . . . and *original*. Gathering ideas from others while still creating work that is unique is a delicate dance, but it's not something to be feared.

Let's delve deeper into this topic . . . together!

ESSAY: Inspiration vs. Plagiarism

It's time to address the elephant in the room: plagiarism. It's a word that definitely gives us all the "ick," but it's something we've got to face when we talk about gathering inspiration for our artwork. We've seen so many of our students and artist peers freeze in their tracks because they're scared of either being plagiarized themselves or inadvertently ripping someone else off. There's a lot of discomfort that comes up around this topic, and we get it. But the best thing we can do to combat the fear is to speak transparently about copying—to define where the lines are as best we can, and to show how thoughtful, ethical inspiration is a really positive tool that should be embraced in your art practice!

First of all, we should get on the same page about what does and doesn't constitute plagiarism. Plagiarism is direct theft. It's taking someone else's hard work and slapping your name on it. It's blatant stealing, and it's pretty darn black and white. We should all agree that this sort of copying is clearly wrong, and it's the antithesis of why we chose to be artists in the first place. We're all out here trying to express our truest selves, so why would we want to hide behind someone else's voice and ideas anyway?

The lines get blurrier, however, when the art in question isn't a direct mirror image of the original. Perhaps one artwork utilizes the same colors and shapes as another, but the composition has been altered. Or maybe a few of the elements are eerily similar, but the medium is different. The question we have to ask ourselves now is: *How different is different enough?*

Here's the thing—if you are simply reading these words, it means that you care about using inspiration ethically. Simply being aware and observant of your own influences and their presence in your work is most of the battle! The reality is that nothing is *truly* original, and honestly that's such a relief. No one is expecting you to pull something out of thin air, free of influence and inspiration from outside sources. We don't live in a vacuum, so there's simply no way to go through life untouched by influences. But why would we want a life like that, even if it *were* possible? The coolest thing about being human is that we get to share it with each other! We're constantly impacting those around us in big and small ways, encouraging growth and change and trial and error. That's life, baby, and it's pretty awesome, if you ask us.

We wish we could give you an exact formula for how much your piece has to veer from another to ensure it's not a copy, but neither art nor life works that way. We can, however, give you some tips and strategies to make sure your own voice is shining through and that your inspirations are taking their proper role as supporting characters in your art.

ETHICAL INSPIRATION GUIDELINES

✱ Look for inspiration from different sources, and remix ideas.

Instead of copying ideas from a single source, try remixing ideas from many different places. A smoothie with one ingredient, like the work of just one artist you admire, would just be . . . a single piece of fruit in a blender? BORING. You can easily jazz up that smoothie and add some flavor by making sure you're incorporating lots of different influences and combining them in surprising ways. Maybe you borrow a color palette from an oil painting you saw in a museum and apply it to a pattern inspired by the drapes that hung in your room as a kid. Or what if you let the lyrics of your favorite song inspire a drawing that also explores a shading technique you found on some old packaging? The more you mix and match influences, the more surprising and exciting the result—and the more confident you'll be that you've cooked up a recipe no one else has ever tried!

Extra hot tip: If your inspiration is mainly coming from art, make sure you're looking at five or more pieces from different artists. Then try limiting the amount of time you allow yourself to look at each one as you're creating your own work. Be mindful of what ideas are springing from each source of inspiration, so you're never pulling too much from any single piece or artist.

✱ Try to keep your inspiration abstract rather than literal when you can.

Instead of emulating or replicating exact imagery from artists you admire, try identifying the *qualities* that you feel drawn to. Is it the sense of mystery that's exciting in their work? Is it the intimacy of the portraits they're painting? Try to dig deeper to find the feelings and emotions you're picking up on, and then experiment with other ways to visually convey those abstract ideas.

✱ Get outside and off your phone!

As convenient as it is to look for cool art by scrolling on social media, we often end up in a loop of content that the algorithm thinks we want to see, so we're never really stepping out of our comfort zone. We're also way more likely to be served up trends that are already overdone, which isn't the best way to get inspired to make something truly exciting and original! Instead, try checking out a museum, a vintage store, a conservatory, or even sitting on the couch listening to your favorite music. Try a craft or art form outside your wheelhouse—look for a local pottery workshop, try photography, or take a weaving class! One of Katie's favorite pastimes is to "deep dive" by doing research on random topics that pique her interest. Whether she's taking a class on quantum physics, bingeing the latest trashy reality TV show, or writing music with her husband, changing her routine and following her curiosity always has positive results. Exploring varying interests is good for your mental health, and it keeps your creative juices flowing long after.

✱ Listen to your gut.

If you're looking at something you made and start to get a bad feeling in the pit of your stomach because it feels a bit too close to your source of inspiration—pay attention to what your body is telling you! Run through the tips we've discussed above and ask yourself if you took those steps, or if you should continue to push your work further from those original influences. If you feel any kind of guilt or shame around your artwork, that's a big ol' red flag telling you to revisit and make sure your inspirations are integrated in an ethical way.

The anti-copying checklist:

- ☑ Pull inspiration from multiple sources and remix it
- ☑ Keep your inspiration abstract
- ☑ Get inspired outside of social media
- ☑ Listen to your gut

While copying and claiming the art as your own is a bad idea, copying art for practice and skill-building can be a very beneficial learning experience. Replicating masterworks is an exercise commonly done in art classes, and we encourage you to try it (we've done it ourselves!). There's so much you can learn from attempting to create the exact result that another artist was able to achieve. *What tools did they use? How did they hold them, and how much pressure did they apply? How did they blend colors to achieve that particular look?* The goal is not to analyze the artwork so you can use all the same techniques in your own work, but to take away bits and pieces from the experience that you can then make your own. Say you saw a watercolor illustration of a horse that you couldn't take your eyes off of. Your first step might be to re-create the horse to learn about how it was constructed. Next, maybe you'll try those techniques with an elephant, and then a flower. Each time, you'll build on your skills and add in more and more of yourself along the way. While copying is a big no for us in almost all situations, this scenario is an exception to the rule!

If your worry is more about others copying *you* than the other way around, we have a few pieces of advice. First, don't allow fear to keep you from making your art—it's not fair to you. We could make up all sorts of potential negative scenarios that could stop us from doing all kinds of things in life, but anxious projections tend to be more harmful than helpful to us in the end (trust Katie on this one—she has panic disorder!). Instead of coming from a place of protectiveness and defensiveness, what would happen if you adopted a more positive outlook and didn't automatically assume the worst? Most likely, a change in attitude won't alter whether someone will actually copy you or not, but it *will* make your emotional load lighter.

In addition to shifting your expectations, there are also some reasonable protections you can put in place should you run into an issue with plagiarism at some point. You could limit the file size of the images of your art that you share online—that way people won't be able to make high-resolution reproductions on their own. You might consider copyrighting your art, which, in the United States, involves paying fees to the US Copyright Office in return for basic protections and the ability to sue copyright violators. You could also go ahead and connect with a copyright lawyer so if you need one later, you're not left scrambling at the last minute. Taking a few protective measures in advance can help you feel prepared so you can focus less on worrying and more on making art!

We included this passage about copying because it's a topic that comes up frequently with our students and we know it's important. The goal isn't to freak you out that someone will copy you, and it's definitely not to scare you away from incorporating influences into your work—in fact, we *encourage you to lean into them!* Inspiration is important, and as long as you're following our tips above and paying attention to how you incorporate your ingredients into your smoothie (don't forget to blend 'em up realllll good), you'll be A-OK.

All this talk about inspiration is getting us excited to go make something already! What do you think, shall we stop chattin' and start doin'?

Let's head into the next chapter and *make some art*!

CHAPTER 3

Creative Adventure

You've done it. You've officially reached the juicy center of this book, and it's time to reap the rewards! We've been asking you to get super introspective and analytical in the past few chapters, and you've hopefully come out on the other side with a better understanding of yourself. But now, it's time to totally switch gears and just PLAY.

Remember play? Think back to being a kid, when you used to make things with your hands for the pure enjoyment of it, and you didn't muddy it all up with the pressure of high expectations or judgments. We're going to channel those vibes, roll up our sleeves, and try to just enjoy creating again.

If the process of finding your creative identity were a sub sandwich, we'd be deep into the meat and cheese of it right about now. As important as the rest of the process is, you can't have a tasty sandwich if you leave out the main components, and you can't find your artistic voice if you don't make a bunch of artwork. Here's the thing, though—not all of the art you make is going to be "good," and that's okay. In fact, we want to encourage you to ditch those perfectionist tendencies you may be harboring and commit to making *imperfect work*, within this book and outside of it. The more free you feel to experiment, even if that means getting messy or being "bad" at first, the more chances you'll have to stumble on something really special. You don't think van Gogh created *Starry Night* the first time he picked up a paintbrush, do you?

We know personally how intimidating a blank canvas can be. When anything is possible, making those initial decisions and putting pen to paper is often the hardest part. If you find yourself overthinking as you approach these prompts, it may help to remove some of the pressure with a change in perspective. What if you thought of every piece you make as a diary entry? That's what record executive and producer Rick Rubin suggests in his book *The Creative Act: A Way of Being*. You're not creating something that needs to be publicly displayed or judged. You're simply taking a snapshot of who you are at one moment in time—a reflection of yourself that's free of expectations. A diary entry isn't "good" or "bad," it's just the true story of who you are right now. That's what we're aiming for here—not perfection, not a performance, but honest, playful exploration.

If you find you're still having difficulty getting into a healthy, judgment-free headspace as you work through this chapter, it's likely stemming from fear, unrealistic expectations, or ideas about yourself that simply aren't true. It's hard work to break through limiting beliefs and all the icky stuff that lurks behind creative block, but we've included lots of tips at the end of this chapter that should give you a leg up. Feel free to press pause on the prompts and take some time to look over our suggestions if you find yourself in a rut (which, we want to remind you, is absolutely part of the process of being an artist!).

FROM KATIE

Friends, I say this with love for whoever needs to hear it: *perfectionism is not a compliment*. As a recovering perfectionist myself, I know firsthand how debilitating striving to be "the best" can be.

At some point in my childhood, I realized that I received praise and attention when I performed at a high level, and I fell into a cycle of trying to prove my worth through my achievements. While on the outside it looked like I was kicking life's butt, inside I was a mess of anxiety and stress, and it all finally boiled over when I left my nine-to-five job to go full-time freelance.

I came face-to-face with the results of all the pressure I had put on myself when I was diagnosed with panic disorder. It has taken many years of therapy, practice, and medication to arrive at a healthier place, and the greatest lesson I've learned is how important the intentional act of *imperfection* can be. Greatness is great because it is *rare*, so expecting greatness from yourself at every turn is simply not possible or sustainable. The more grace we give ourselves, the more room we create for greatness to come in . . . when it's ready.

Now—take a moment to release the tension in your body. Let your shoulders drop. Unclench your jaw. Remind yourself that this is *your* time and nobody else's. Turn on your favorite music and really set the vibe. Then, when you feel your body relaxing and your mindset clicking into place, pick up your pencil, or a dried-up marker, or your kid's broken crayon. Sometimes the "wrong" tool makes this step feel more exploratory and less intimidating.

Let's dig in and have some fun!

Serious art is born from serious play.

Julia Cameron

THE CREATIVE ADVENTURE

1. **Don't take yourself, these prompts, or the work that comes out of you too seriously. This is a time for exploration, play, and getting in touch with the joy of making. There is literally no possibility of failure here.**

2. **Try to come from a mindset of experimentation and curiosity. Ask yourself, "What if I tried it this way?" but don't overthink it. Allow your subconscious mind to do its work.**

3. **Use your inner voice as your compass. Don't make anything because you think it's the "right answer." Do it because it feels good, because it makes you laugh, because it strikes a chord, or because it is fun. Pay attention to when you're enjoying yourself the most.**

4. **Let go of expectations. Remember these are honest reflections of you, right now, and not a performance. You showed up, and that's what counts.**

WHAT YOU'LL NEED

For these exercises, you can use whatever materials you like or have on hand. Get creative and try some different things! You can create right here in this book, or you can work separately on a tablet, a sketchbook, or wherever feels most comfortable for you today. Remember, whichever approach you choose to take is the right one—this is about self-discovery, after all.

It's up to you how much time you'd like to spend on each prompt. Learning how long you like to focus when you're creating is part of the process, too. Don't feel any pressure to complete these in one sitting; they'll be here when you need them!

How Do You Doodle

Doodle for ten minutes straight. Don't think about it. Let your hand flow and fully zen out while listening to your favorite music or podcast. Scribbling is encouraged!

Draw from Memory

Pick an animal and try to draw it from memory (like a giraffe or a kangaroo, for example). No references allowed, NO cheating. If you're anything like us, it's going to end up looking pretty darn wonky. EMBRACE THE WONK!

Finish the Drawing

Complete the image we've started here however you like.

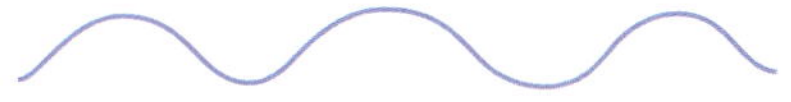

Unusual Tool

Use a tool that's not meant for art-making
(e.g., Wite-Out, lipstick) to create an illustration.

Something Old

Find one of your old sketches, a jotted-down note, or some half-finished thing and use it as inspiration for an illustration. Bring it back to life and give it a new energy!

Something New

Draw something that is totally imagined and doesn't exist in real life.

Something Borrowed

Go outside and grab some twigs, leaves, flowers . . . anything. Then arrange them into an interesting composition. You can draw it, glue it down, take a photo, etc.

Something Blue

Create an abstract composition (focus on shapes and lines) and use only the color blue.

To the Limit

What choices will you make when faced with different limitations? Pick an item that's within your view and draw it four different times, using a new set of limitations each time from the instructions below.

1. Use only two or three colors.

2. Make it small enough to fit in the box below.

3. Don't use any curved lines.

4. Draw it upside-down (no rotating the page!).

Surface Level

Draw an apple three times, each time experimenting with a different way of rendering texture.

In the Deep

Draw something you'd find at the bottom of the ocean.

Mundane to Exciting

Pick a boring everyday object (like a stapler, the TV remote, etc.) and spice things up! Use really vibrant colors, turn it into a character with a personality, or come up with another way to make it way more interesting.

Draw It Wrong

Draw something you see right now, but draw it wrong. Maybe the perspective isn't accurate or the scale is completely off.

Contour This

1. Draw an object (or a person) you see, without picking up your pen off the paper. Make it one continuous line to create some interesting experiments.

2. Now draw the same thing again, but do it with your eyes closed. This means you're not allowed to look at your paper until you're finished!

Good Enough to Eat

Decorate this cake.

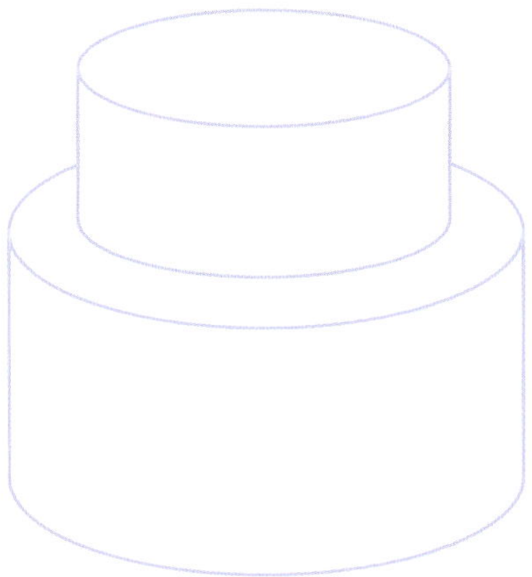

Design Your Collection

If you were to design a collection of flowerpots and vases, what would they look like?

Transcribe the Vibe

Put a song you love on repeat and try to pull the feeling that it gives you into your work.

Ornamentation

Fill in these boxes with different types of “space-filling” ornaments or details. This could be foliage, shapes, dots, swirls, etc.

Time Travel

Pick a period from art history (mid-century modern, impressionist, art nouveau, etc.) and create a sticker sheet that represents that era. Obviously, stickers weren't around in olden times . . . so *use your imaginations, people!*

Set the Mood

Pick a mood, then draw a tree in a way that conveys that mood (sad, excited, angry, scared, etc.).

Adjective Play

Create three different drawings. Each should represent one of the following adjectives . . .

1. Noisy

2. Spicy

3. Cozy

Draw a Map of YOU

Create an illustrated "map" or "guide" to show people who you are. Include words, symbols, or illustrations that represent your most important features, likes, or personality pillars. (For example, Katie's would represent art nouveau, reality TV, pink, pasta, sci-fi books, etc.!)

We sincerely hope you've had a blast working through these creative prompts and that you unearthed some interesting ideas along the way! Take a second to assess whatever feelings are coming up. Are you excited by what you created? Surprised? Did you feel more free to experiment as you went on, or did you find it difficult to really let go? Take stock of your emotions (but try not to judge them) and then give yourself a big ol' pat on the back for digging in and doing the work!

Remember, this is absolutely not the last time you should set aside time for creative play! As artists, it's *so* important to regularly give yourself space to experiment and reconnect with who you really are as a creator. You're always evolving as a person, which means your artwork will evolve, too! Make sure to schedule in time to revisit these prompts (or to create new ones on your own) perhaps every quarter, or at least every year, to see how your responses change. Set a date in your calendar right now so you don't forget! These exercises are great to come back to when you find yourself uninspired, tapped out, or stuck, too.

Our number-one suggestion for artists who want to grow in their craft and understand themselves better is to make, make, make. Make art and then make more art! However, we know that's much easier said than done. We're not machines; we can't just press a button and pop out a masterpiece! As we mentioned earlier in this chapter, there's so much junk that can clog up our creativity—from perfectionism to burnout to lack of inspiration. So, let's take some time to delve into the strategies we've gathered over the years to combat these annoying obstacles and keep our creative juices flowing, even when it's hard.

IF YOU'RE MAKING AN EFFORT, IT WILL NEVER COME BACK VOID.

HOODZPAH DESIGN

ESSAY: How to Get Unstuck

If you've ever sat down to create something only to find yourself feeling overwhelmed, lost, or even just totally out of ideas, you're not alone! Unfortunately, getting "stuck" every once in a while is just par for the course when you're an artist. Sometimes it's a case of creative block, and other times it's fear rearing its head. Maybe it's exhaustion, or Mercury in retrograde, or just a bump in the road you didn't expect. It happens to everyone, and while it definitely isn't fun to experience any of these obstacles, each hurdle is ultimately a stepping stone for growth.

When you're in a creative slump, it can feel like you'll never get out. But we promise, there's light on the other side! Let's examine some of the most common reasons why we get stuck and work through some strategies we've developed over the years to get the inspiration flowing again.

✱ You're uninspired.

If your creative spark is burning on low and you're lacking the excitement you usually feel when you make art, you might just be in need of an inspiration refresh! Remember earlier in this book when we talked about how the stuff you're looking at and surrounding yourself with on a daily basis has a huge impact on the art you make? Well, this is where that idea really comes into play. Sure, you may spend hours every day consuming content via various social platforms, but it's not the *quantity* of inputs that will fill your creative tank back up—it's the *quality* that makes the biggest impact. The first thing we recommend doing is switching up where you're currently searching for inspiration. If you're a chronic scroller like us (guilty!), that means it's a good time to *put your darn phone down!* Your social feed is probably not going to help you get your spark back . . . so, let's find you something that will!

Try focusing on your environment first. Can you change something about your surroundings? This doesn't require a week-long trip to a new city in a luxury hotel (that does sound fun, though!), but maybe trying a new coffee shop, visiting an antique store, or working outside instead of inside will change your perspective enough to open up some new creative pathways. Or maybe it's time to break out the old overalls, throw some headphones on, and paint your bedroom that outrageous color you've been thinking about. Sometimes, just making time to get quiet and listen to ourselves is enough. We often have our best ideas as we're falling asleep or taking a long shower, when the noise of our daily lives isn't as distracting.

You can also try giving yourself a fun new challenge—something that will flex your mental muscles and encourage you to change your thought patterns. Sign up for a class to learn a new skill, for example. Trying something out of left field, like a glassblowing workshop, might be just the thing you need. Whether it's completing a puzzle, listening to an audiobook about a topic you know nothing about, or finally reorganizing your closet, any activity that stretches your brain in a new way is helpful when you're trying to grease your creative wheels.

✱ You're burned out.
You're exhausted. You've been working overtime (either mentally or physically), and your body is craving rest, so you'd better listen. We find that burnout usually rears its head at the most inconvenient times, when you have so much to do that taking a break feels impossible. But if you don't take some time to recover, you risk doing a crap job (or worse yet, really hurting yourself). Your creative muscles need a chance to heal so they can rebuild stronger than before.

It's normal to need to recharge your batteries once in a while, but if you find you're often running on an empty tank, it's time to figure out what you need to change to help you feel better and healthier. We know a thing or two about burnout (been there, done that!), but learning to pay attention to the early signs has really helped because it gives us an opportunity to act before things start to go too far downhill. For us, signs of burnout look like: avoiding or procrastinating on tasks, low energy, mood swings, anxiety, and depression. Typically, these signs will show up in small ways at first, like getting unusually frustrated when the refrigerator door gets stuck or needing naps a little too often. Pay attention to what your early signs are so you can begin to recognize them and intervene before things get *really* bad.

When you do identify symptoms of burnout, prioritizing rest and revival is critical. Taking some time for yourself is a great place to start. Depending on how much space you need, you might even have to ask for help (gasp!) to rearrange your schedule. Maybe you need someone to cover a meeting for you. Perhaps offloading a particularly stressful project will help most. Maybe you need to stay home from an event or hire a virtual assistant for a while. Take stock of what your body and mind need, and *prioritize that*. Your health always comes first, and work will be there when you get back.

It may sound counterintuitive when all you want to do is become one with your couch, but moving your body and getting some fresh air are vital during your recovery time. Grab your headphones and blast your favorite album while you walk the dog, or just listen to the birds chirping. If you can,

compete externally and you compare

compete internally and you improve

JAMES CLEAR

take a stroll along the beach and bury your feet in the sand. Ground yourself in something that brings you joy and peace.

While these tips and tricks are helpful for combating occasional burnout, you may need to make even bigger changes in your life if you're feeling this way too often. Is your schedule simply too demanding? Then maybe you need to drop something entirely from your plate. Is your work environment toxic? Maybe it's time to go job hunting. While it's scary to make big moves like these, it's so important to remember we have the power to change things that aren't working for us, even if it's hard. Future you will *always* be happy when you prioritize your health and happiness.

✱ You're stuck in a comparison trap.

It has been said before, but it bears repeating: Comparison truly is the thief of joy (thank you, Theodore Roosevelt, or whoever said this first). We get that it's incredibly difficult to separate yourself from what other people are doing and accomplishing, especially in the era of social media, follower counts, and blue check marks. But we have to remember that we're all in very different places in our lives, and we're all facing very different circumstances. Pardon the cliché, but someone else's success doesn't diminish yours. And you should never compare your beginning with someone else's middle. We just want to be happy, and that journey looks totally different for every single one of us!

Instead of wishing you could make art like someone else, concentrate on the stuff you do that sets *you* apart, and lean in. Not sure what your unique attributes are? Well, try reading this book to help you find out! There's always some idea, some way of perceiving, some brilliantly, weirdly wonderful way you experience the world that sets you apart. And that genius is going to come out only when you create art from a place of authenticity, not when you're trying to replicate someone else's special sauce. We know we sound like your mom, but it's true. You can do it; just be yourself!

OVERWHELM AND DECISION PARALYSIS

Because you're creative in the depths of your soul, you likely have a *lot* of ideas! It can feel really overwhelming to try to figure out where to start and how to manage your time if you're tackling too many at once. If you try to implement all the ideas at the same time, you'll inevitably find yourself juggling a ton of cracked eggs. You're much more likely to keep your eggs intact when you focus on just a few of them.

So, how do you decide which ideas and projects to prioritize?

PROJECT PRIORITIZATION

Start by making a list of the current ideas, projects, and aspirations that are floating around in your head. From there, you'll pick your top three to focus on by using the scorecard below. For every idea you have, simply ask yourself each question on the scorecard and then give it a rating from 1 to 5. When you've finished scoring, total up the results, and the top three highest scores win! (Feel free to change or add questions based on your own goals and priorities.)

✱ SCORECARD (rate each project idea from 1 to 5)

PROJECT NAME	How much fun will I have?	Does this move the needle forward for my career goals?	How much money will this make (if any)?	How fast can I get it done?	TOTAL SCORE
Project Example	*3*	*4*	*2*	*4*	*13*

you
are
complete
but
you
are
not
finished.

Still excited about all your potential projects and can't seem to narrow them down? Try putting all the ideas in a hat and picking one. It's better to put pencil to paper than to freeze and make nothing. You won't always pick the "best" idea, and this exercise might help you come to peace with that. It's the hat's fault!

Procrastination is yet another roadblock we use to get in our own way. When you find yourself saying, "I can't do X until I do Z," or better yet, "I can't do Z until I've done the whole alphabet" . . . *you* might be the bottleneck! If you're putting off "doing the thing" because you need to do all the other things first, or you need a bigger audience, or more skills, it's a good time to reflect and figure out why you're stopping yourself from making progress. First, make sure you're *truly* excited about the idea and not just doing it because you think it's what you're *supposed* to do. If that's not the issue, it may very well be fear that's stopping you in your tracks.

Let's take a deeper look into how we can handle that scenario.

✱ You're scared.

Fear is a feisty little sucker that holds so many artists back. When fear tries to take the wheel and keep us from creating, we like to combat it by actually thinking through the worst-case scenario. So . . . someone doesn't like your work? That's just part of being an artist, and it's totally okay (encouraged, in fact!) to make art that's not for everyone. Having a point of view that doesn't jive with one group makes our work even more special for the folks who *do* get it.

Rejection of any kind is hard, which is why we have to practice it. Yep, that's right—we have to get good at hearing "no" and facing criticism, and part of that process means learning when to listen as well as when to totally tune it out. We've heard people say "Don't take criticism from someone you wouldn't ask for advice," and that feels like a pretty darn good measuring stick to use. Ultimately, making art is about *you* and the audience you're speaking to, and those are the only people whose opinions should really matter.

Whatever the reason fear pops up for you, you cannot let it dim your light. It may sound a little woo-woo, but the world absolutely needs your gift. Imagine if your art makes someone smile, makes them feel seen, teaches them something, or inspires them in some way . . . aren't those great reasons to kick fear to the curb and keep creating? Plus, the act of making art is literally therapy, and it's often much less expensive (but seriously, *real* therapy helps too).

THE GAP

There's a "gap" in every creative journey that isn't talked about enough—a divide that separates an artist's vision from what they're actually able to create. The gap happens when your skill level doesn't yet match your taste, and you're left feeling frustrated because your work doesn't look exactly like you want it to. When you don't have the technical ability to achieve the aesthetic you're aiming for, it can leave you feeling defeated. Ira Glass, a popular American radio personality, has spoken about this gap at length, noting that it often leads people to doubt that they will ever become as good as they want to be and causes artists with incredible potential to stop in their tracks before they ever really get started.

The antidote? Fight past those fears and keep going. You just haven't made enough work yet. You haven't put in your hypothetical ten thousand hours (the amount of practice time Malcolm Gladwell famously suggested you need to become truly great at something), and you're just giving up too soon! It may not take *exactly* ten thousand hours to become an expert, but the point is . . . it's not something that's going to magically happen overnight. We see so many aspiring artists throw in the towel before they ever really give themselves a chance. The trick is to figure out how to enjoy the process, because that's all we've got! There is no point at which you'll reach the peak. Even the most skilled artists always have room to grow and evolve. So, sit back, get comfy, and have fun experimenting and learning, because the process is the destination.

CHAPTER 4

Reflecting & Putting the Pieces Together

Grab your detective hat, because we're about to go full-on Sherlock Holmes. We're going to search through all the work you did in the previous chapters to find the trends, consistencies, and throughlines within your art and personality. Everything we've done up to this point has been laying the puzzle pieces out on the table, and now we're going to start putting them together. It's time to connect the dots and form a clearer picture of who you are as an artist!

The reason we're on this treasure hunt through your psyche in the first place is because we're looking for the qualities that make you unique. We want to hone in on the traits that make you memorable and find the parts of your story that people can connect with, because it's so much easier to find your true fans when your audience can really *know* you. Plus, you'll feel more fulfilled as a creator when you have a clear direction and a deeper understanding of yourself.

Remember, this work is about uncovering who you *already are* and leaning into the creative superpowers you *already possess.*

If you ever feel like you're forcing anything, pretending to be someone you're not, or you're pushing yourself in an artistic direction that seems inauthentic—that's a big red flag telling you you're heading in the wrong direction and it's time to turn the ship around!

It's totally okay to dip your toe into something to test the waters and then decide later that it just doesn't feel right. For example, maybe you've noticed you have some maximalist tendencies while completing the exercises in this book, and you decide to try amplifying those qualities even more to see how it feels. But once you put that into practice, you realize it just doesn't feel right. You may also find that there are plenty of things you enjoy and appreciate but ultimately just want to admire from afar; not everything that inspires you has to become part of your aesthetic or personality. This phase of identifying your distinctive characteristics is never complete, and you'll find yourself trying some attributes on for size that you end up ditching later on. That's completely normal—so common, in fact, that we'll talk about it even more later in this chapter.

If you're new to the art world, or you find yourself lacking confidence in your skills, you may struggle with this section of the book. We're asking you to define your voice, and that's a difficult thing to do if you're not creating work that you're really excited about yet! We mentioned this before when we spoke about creative block—there might just be a gap between your taste level (which is high!) and what your skill level will let you actually achieve right now. That gap is something we all face as we're learning, and it understandably causes a lot of frustration. If you're nodding along with all of this, don't give up! Keep practicing, trying new things, and make more of the art that feels fun and exciting. As you work through the following exercises, try your best to identify some of the qualities that are beginning to emerge, but leave room to grow. You'll definitely want to revisit this part of the book as you start to feel more sure of your work.

Now, without further ado, let's stop talking and start doing!

THERE IS NO PATH. THE PATH IS MADE BY WALKING

Antonio Machado

DESCRIBING YOUR ARTWORK

First, you'll need to flip back to the exercises you just completed in the Creative Adventure chapter (pages 63–77). Take some time to look over each piece of work you created, and **write down words or phrases in the margins or on another sheet of paper that describe what you made.** Remember, this isn't about judging the art you created as "good" or "bad," it's about identifying the qualities that make the work *yours* and not someone else's. More specific and distinctive words are best, as they paint a clearer picture of how you differ from other artists. For example, instead of saying your work is "fun," you might dig deeper to words like "joyful," "unrestrained," or "eccentric." It may help to have a thesaurus nearby!

Consider each of the following categories as you're coming up with descriptive words: color, texture, shape, perspective, line work, rhythm and movement, composition, hierarchy, and subject matter. (You can revisit the Elements of Art Glossary on page 43 if you need a refresher on what these terms mean.)

Some examples of words or phrases you might use to describe your art could be: *precise*, *jewel tones*, *repetition*, *exaggeration*, *lots of negative space*, *soothing*, etc.

Try not to edit yourself or overthink too much yet. This is just a brainstorming exercise! If you get stuck, head back to page 44 to see the words we used to express other artists' creative identities.

CREATE YOUR WORD BANK

Once you've finished brainstorming, it's time to move on to the next phase of our analysis. Grab a highlighter or your favorite colorful pen. In this exercise, you'll **revisit the words you just came up with** about your work as well as the prompts you completed in chapter 2 (Getting to Know Yourself). As you do this, **circle or highlight words and phrases that really stand out**, that feel particularly truthful and authentic, or that you notice appearing multiple times. Then, **transfer your favorite fifteen to twenty words or phrases** to the "My Word Bank" box below. These words can express your biggest influences, hallmarks of your particular aesthetic, subjects or messages that you gravitate toward, or anything else that helps paint the picture of who you are and the art that you make.

If your creative identity is a smoothie, this word bank describes the flavor. We're finally figuring out what results when all of your experiences, influences, preferences, and personality traits mix together! And in the next chapter, you'll find even more clarity as you learn how to share your unique flavor blend with the world.

Here's a quick reference for where you can find those previous exercises:

- **Getting to Know Yourself prompts: pages 31–40**
- **Mood board: pages 37–38**
- **Creative Adventure prompts: pages 63–77**

✳ MY WORD BANK

....

....

....

....

....

....

YOU CAN'T

— READ

THE LABEL

FROM —

— INSIDE

THE JAR —

FROM ILANA

I've got to be honest—this section is the hardest for me.

If there's anywhere I overthink and seek external validation, it's right here. As someone who's typically tackling tasks quickly and methodically, backing up to see the big picture often feels really challenging. I know that's true for lots of us artist types, because we're used to being so close to our work (who else is guilty of working while zoomed in 700 percent on your computer?). But, as they say, you can't read the label when you're inside the jar. Sometimes, we need help seeing ourselves and our work from a broader perspective—that's why asking for help is such a powerful tool. Just remember, when you do ask others to weigh in and give you feedback about your art, you get to choose whose opinion you value.

While writing this book, I really struggled to define my own creative identity (the irony!). I had most of the puzzle pieces, but I couldn't seem to fit them together. Katie helped me zoom out, spot the throughlines in my work, and see the strengths I couldn't recognize on my own.

As you go through the "Create Your Word Bank" exercise, you may find yourself hesitating to commit to certain descriptors. What if you don't want to be known as the artist who uses "jewel tones" forever? What if you identify with some traits now, but change later down the line? It's absolutely normal to evolve as a person and an artist. In fact, change is an inevitable part of life that we should embrace with open arms! The words you're choosing now are indicative of who you are at this moment, but they're absolutely not set in stone.

When we work one-on-one with students to help them uncover their creative identities, this topic of allowing for personal evolution is usually where they struggle the most. How do we define and narrow in on our creative identities *now* while still allowing room to evolve later on? How do we find a concise way to describe our art when we are interested in so many different things?

These are great questions that deserve some thorough answers. Let's dive in!

ESSAY: The Evolution of YOU

At this point in the book, we hope it's pretty clear that there are some important benefits to consistency as an artist. You may have even thought to yourself, *Sheesh . . . do these women ever shut up about through-lines?* We may be guilty of harping on the subject, but that's only because it's so important. When you find and celebrate the threads that tie all your work together, your artistic vision becomes sharper, and others find it *so much easier* to understand and get excited about what you do as well.

However, as creative folks who are naturally pulled to explore, try new things, and experiment, "consistency" can sound like a mighty scary word. Attempting to define who we are while also constantly experiencing personal growth and change is confusing, and there are lots of doubts and fears that bubble up. Let's put them all out in the open so we can work through them together.

✱ I don't want to be put in a box.

We totally get that you need room to be your complex, curious, ever-changing self, and we *want* you to have that space! So, take a deep breath and a sigh of relief, because we'd never suggest that you need to confine yourself to one style or medium for the rest of your days to be successful. Consistency can take a million different forms, and the patterns that unify your work will be totally different from those that unify someone else's. One person's portfolio might be cohesive because all the pieces depict the magic of seemingly mundane, everyday moments. Another artist's work might focus on all aerial photography. And a third artist might draw many different subjects but always using outlines to define the shapes and characters. We'll talk more about how to define *your* consistencies in the next chapter, but the point for now is: YOU get to define how broad or narrow your unifying characteristics will be, so don't panic!

As we explained earlier in this book, it's also completely okay to be an artist who has multiple styles. In chapter 1, we defined the difference between your *creative identity* and your *style*. We imagined that your creative identity is like an ice cream shop, and a style is just one flavor in that shop. Your creative identity is the sum of who you are and all the intricacies that make you special. A style is just ONE way that you might express that identity aesthetically. Artists are allowed to not only change their style over time, but also play with multiple styles at the *same* time. Listen to yourself and give yourself permission to be the artist *you* want to be.

✱ I struggle to find consistency in my work.

If you're feeling overwhelmed by how diverse your portfolio is, you might want to break it into sections and try reframing different periods of exploration in your work as "collections." Artists often organize their ventures into new styles, mediums, or subject matter simply by separating them into a new category within their larger body of work. Think about how a fashion designer releases different collections, for example. One collection might feature evening gowns with lots of glitz and glam, and the next might showcase more casual resort wear and swimsuits. Each collection has the designer's unique stamp on it, but they highlight different materials, ideas, and contexts. Did you know that Picasso, known for his cubism and collage work, also painted realism portraits? Mary GrandPré, who illustrated the US Scholastic *Harry Potter* covers, has also created beautiful abstract art. Many successful artists have worked in collections or have embraced different "eras" of change while still creating memorable, recognizable work. You can do it, too!

If you simply can't seem to find any unifying traits at all, consider that, ironically, experimentation could be one of the consistencies that ties your work together. You might become known as someone who is always trying new things and exploring new mediums. One of Katie's favorite singers, Kimbra, is notorious for experimenting with lots of different genres. In a songwriting workshop that Katie took, Kimbra explained that her audience has come to expect the unexpected, and that she attracts listeners who enjoy being surprised. She is daring and unafraid to push her music in unusual ways, and those qualities have become central to her brand.

And finally, don't forget to ask a friend for help if you're having trouble seeing your throughlines. We've mentioned before that getting out of your own head and asking for someone else's perspective might be all it takes to find your breakthrough.

✱ I feel like I have to hide parts of myself if I want to appear consistent.

Have you kept important parts of your life or personality hidden because you feel they don't "fit" into your "artist" persona? You might be surprised to find that embracing and sharing those pieces of yourself could actually help differentiate you (plus, you'll feel more honest and authentic in the process)!

Creatives often think they'll overwhelm or confuse people if they share a quirk or unexpected interest that's not directly related to the art they usually make. But we've found that our audiences are often even *more* engaged when we talk about the other things we love. Katie's DMs light up when she posts about her DIY interior design projects, and Ilana's salad selfies are some of her most popular content. Go figure! You don't owe people all of you (or anything, for that matter), but don't be afraid to let them see beyond the surface if there's something you want to share.

You can help your audience connect the dots about anything that excites you simply by telling them your story with confidence. Take our friend Elizabeth Gray (@thegraytergood on Instagram), for example. She's a self-proclaimed "artist, illustrator, muralist, and nail girlie." At first, you might think that nail art is a little out of left field, but when you actually see how she incorporates it, it makes tons of sense and only gives her a more distinctive perspective as an artist. Elizabeth shares process videos of the gorgeous, intricate designs she hand-paints on her nails, and then gives them even more screen time when they appear in her iconic overhead shots of her lettering work. Because she has featured her nail art and talked about it with her audience, she has become a bit of a "nail influencer" and artist in one! Brands ask to work with her specifically to tap into this unique blend of traits, and her social media following has skyrocketed. And all of this happened simply because she wasn't afraid to tell people more of the story of who she is.

✱ I'm afraid to lose followers if I try new things.

When you do become known for something, whether it's a style, a unique use of a medium, or something else entirely, it can be scary to change paths later down the road. The fear of losing followers or disappointing customers and collectors often makes creators hesitant to try new things. In reality, you'll hone in more on your true fans only when you allow yourself to experiment. Showing new sides of yourself will attract people who appreciate you as a whole, complex person, and that's the audience that will become your biggest cheerleaders and clients in the end! No one expects you to grow in only one direction—that would be so boring! The Swifties (Taylor Swift fans) know that each album has a different tone, unique emotions, and sometimes a totally different genre. Not every Swiftie likes country music, but they still sing along to every word of Taylor's breakout country album. They're in it for the journey, and they'll follow Taylor wherever she goes.

Personal evolution is vital to staying creative and inspired, so make room for it! We've grown in lots of ways as creatives throughout our lives, and one of the most important changes has been learning to appreciate imperfection. In design school, we learned a lot about grid systems. As we laid the foundations for our understanding of art, we fixated on staying within the lines, making tidy work, and erasing mistakes (and picking dried rubber cement out of the carpet, but those are stories for another book). But there's a trope that says, "learn the rules so you can break them," and it's a cliché for a reason: because it's true! While it was so important to learn the fundamentals, it wasn't until years later that we both found ways to add much more personality into our pieces by incorporating texture and embracing the natural imperfections that occur when anything is truly handmade! That's when we began to really see our voices shine.

Learning to loosen up over time is something that lots of creatives experience, including Katie's dad, a professional timpanist (a timpani is an instrument in the drum family). When Katie asked him to describe the biggest lesson he learned in his journey to find his voice as a musician, he quickly replied that it was discovering when and how to take creative liberties. When he was younger, he was very rigid about learning to play music exactly as it was written. With maturity, he discovered that he could unlock much more emotion by adding his own interpretations. This is a perfect reminder that drills come before skills! The confidence to color outside the lines and follow the beat of your own drum (literally) comes with time, practice, and from being around other inspiring creatives. But no matter how you arrive at this conclusion, we all eventually realize that real beauty and creativity is found by simply telling our own stories.

No matter who you are, your story is rich, complex, and always evolving.

Whenever you build a new skill or find an exciting new interest, it's like putting on a cozy new layer on a cold day. The consistencies that we're searching for will be there naturally—you don't need to force them, simply to uncover them. So, embrace the change, share your truth, and let people enjoy the full picture of you. That's what being an artist is all about!

CHAPTER 5

Your Artist Statement

You've been on a wild ride learning new things about yourself, experimenting, and reflecting. Props to you for sticking with it and trusting the process so far! Identifying your unique characteristics and finding the words to describe them is a *huge* milestone in this journey, so make sure to treat yo'self to something fun or tasty to celebrate your progress (we assume you must be pretty hungry by now, considering all the food metaphors we've been using).

This chapter is all about finding your unique space in the creative world based on the foundational attributes you've uncovered about yourself. You'll write an artist statement that represents the full picture of your own creative identity and allows you to confidently and succinctly communicate it to others. Talking about your own work is a huge hang-up for so many creatives, but it's so important! If you're feeling hesitant or overwhelmed by the idea, just know you're not alone, and we're here to guide you through the uncomfortable and vulnerable emotions that'll likely come up.

As artists, sharing our work is part of the job description. We can't find clients and buyers, make deep connections, or reach our true fans without putting our art into the world, and that can be a pretty scary thing to do! As the creators of our work, we often feel personally connected to how people respond to it. We're exposing ourselves to feedback, positive *and* negative, and because we put so much of ourselves into what we create, that can make us feel exposed and unsafe.

> ***What if someone doesn't like my art? Does that mean they don't like me? Does it mean I'm not good enough, or that I should change something about myself?***

These are normal fears to have, and unfortunately, we can't promise you they'll ever totally go away. Even the most successful artists still grapple with self-doubt. Part of the work of being a creative is learning how to manage these feelings when they arise—how to find peace in who you are and stand by what you create, even if some people may not understand it. Actually, the internal battle for self-acceptance is something all people face, whether they are artists or not! This is a heavy topic, and it requires a lot of thought, so we'll spend more time on it later in the chapter. But for now, we'd like to offer some perspective on why it's important not to let these worries paralyze you and keep you from putting yourself out there.

Let's shift our mindsets for a minute. Instead of focusing on what happens if people don't resonate with your work, let's try thinking about what happens if they *do*. When you share your art, your story, and your unique perspective, you open yourself up to make genuine human connections. You're giving people a chance to peek behind the curtain and learn something about who you are. When people appreciate or relate to what you've shared, whether it makes them laugh, brings them comfort, shows them a new way of thinking, or something else entirely, they're much more likely to interact and take a follow-up action in response. Maybe they'll follow you and comment on your social post or send you a DM. Maybe they'll send your portfolio link to a friend or save it for later. Maybe they'll buy one of your pieces or hire you for a project. When we give people an opportunity to connect with us and our art, we not only create space for relationships to form, but we attract the clients and customers who see the real value in what we make. Those are the people who will be your *true* fans and supporters and who will ultimately invest in your work.

Remember, we've spent a lot of time uncovering your *already existing* unique characteristics and traits because we believe authenticity is the foundation for everything else. Pretending to be someone you're not, or making art that doesn't feel true to you just because it's trendy and might attract some likes on social media, isn't a sustainable way to approach your career as an artist. If you're looking for fulfillment and happiness, it's definitely not going to come from suppressing the person you are at your core! Be YOU—we can *assure* you that you are good enough just as you are, and you don't need any gimmicks to make connections with people.

Finding Your Niche

We've got one more step for you to take before we dive into writing your artist statement. We're going to find your niche! It's a tricky word to pronounce ("neesh"? "nitch"?), but no matter how you say it, defining it is an important part of this process. Your niche is your specific, unique space in the art world.

NO ONE CAN COMPETE WITH YOU ON BEING YOU

Naval Ravikant

It's a way of approaching your work that you can become known for and that you can "own" as your specialty. Finding a niche gives you focus and clarity about what you should make next, and it tells people what kind of work they can expect from you. (And what, exactly, they should hire you for!)

We've talked your ear off about the importance of consistency and explained that consistency as an artist does *not* have to mean "restriction." It's probably a good time to reiterate this idea. We promise, we're not asking you to make one very specific type of art for the rest of your life! We're just looking to narrow things down a little bit, and there are a *lot* of ways you can approach that.

While most marketing specialists in the business world use the phrase "niche down" to encourage companies to find one very narrow lane within their industry that they can stick to, we like to take a different approach. Artists need room to grow, experiment, and evolve. That's why we prefer the words "niche OUT" instead.

> ***"Niching out" means first honing in on what makes you unique and special, and then applying those characteristics to everything you do.***

So, instead of picking one tiny definition for the art you want to make, like, "I make art for children's books," you might prefer to focus on *the way you approach your art*, like, "I make vibrant lettering that makes words exciting for kids." Reframing your niche in this way allows you to make art that extends outside of the picture book world while still being really clear on who you are and where you shine.

Now, if the idea of only working on children's books sounds perfect for you, that's great too! If you want to hyper-focus on a niche, just make sure that there's a big enough client base for you to make the income or hit the goals you're aiming for. We've seen so many artists get hung up on the idea of being known for only one thing and then

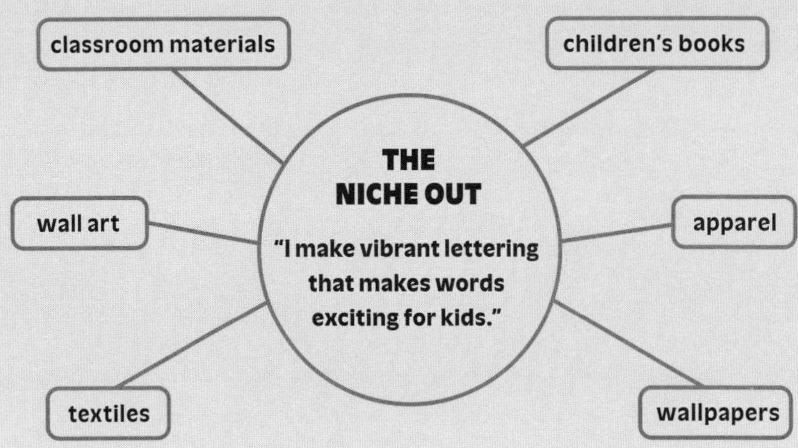

burning out or compromising the other stuff that they love, so we wanted to address how you might avoid that.

Here are some other examples of niches to get your wheels turning:

- An artist who specializes in scientific nature illustrations
- A photographer who focuses on experimental self portraits
- A painter who creates art on tiny canvases
- A hand-lettering artist with a gritty, nineties-grunge-inspired style

As you can see, these niches tie each artist's body of work together in very different ways, but they all convey some sense of consistency that makes it easy to identify that person's art versus someone else's. It's up to you to decide what *your* thread of consistency will be. Will you really zoom in and focus on just one type of art, like the scientific nature illustrator? Will you let your identifiable style be your throughline, like the nineties-grunge-inspired lettering artist? Will your medium or canvas be your differentiator, like the painter who makes art on tiny canvases?

At this point, you're probably wondering how someone comes up with their niche in the first place. Great question! Since your niche should utilize the special traits and characteristics you've already identified in this book, we're going to start brainstorming using those.

PASSION MASH-UP

In this exercise, we're going to mix and match your various passions as well as the key defining words you listed in your word bank in the last chapter (page 93). The goal here is to find a niche that combines the things you love and adds your unique perspective on top.

First, **list things you're passionate about** in the spaces below (cooking, dogs, mountain biking, science, reality TV, etc.). Then, **add your favorite words from your word bank to the list**. Finally, brainstorm ways to **combine the words to create different potential niches**.

Examples:

1. Artist who loves cooking and working with their hands → Niche = creates art using food as the subject matter or even as the medium
2. Painter who loves thrifting and upcycling → Niche = customizes hand-painted vintage apparel
3. Graphic designer who loves movies and collects vintage design → Niche = graphic and prop designer for films

*Fun fact: Katie's husband, Jared, found the career path he's on now by doing this exercise! He put his love for music and video games together, and now he's a sound designer for video games. So cool!

PASSIONS AND KEY WORDS

✱ NICHE IDEAS

Once you have some niche ideas flowing from this exercise that you're excited about, we love to use a Japanese concept called ikigai (translated roughly to "reason for being") to help test them for viability. This is not necessarily the original purpose ikigai was intended for, but we've found it's a really helpful approach to make sure your niche is setting you up for all-around success.

THE IKIGAI TEST

The ikigai diagram looks for the intersection of four things: what you love, what you're good at, what people need, and what you can make money doing (should that be one of your goals). Your niche should live right at the center where they all overlap.

Test your favorite niche ideas from the passion mash-up exercise by seeing if they would fit into the center of the ikigai diagram. Are you good at it (or ready to put in the work to become good at it)? Do people need it? Do you love it? Can you make money from it? (Feel free to omit the money-making question if that's not important to you.)

If the answer is yes to all these questions, congratulations! This might be the right niche for you!

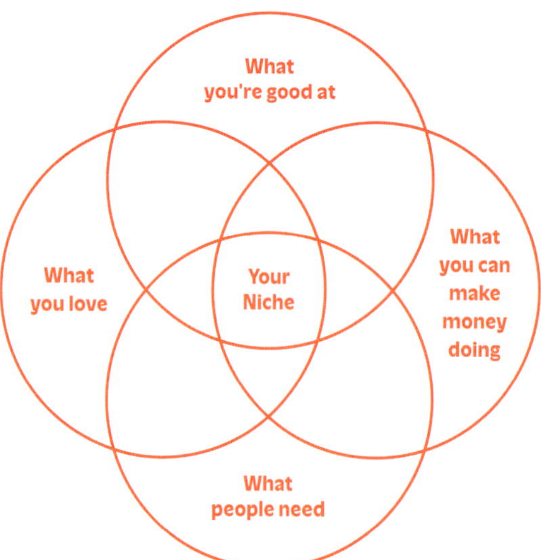

Is It Really a Niche?

Do you have an interesting idea, but you're wondering if it's actually a niche? Here are some questions you can ask yourself to check:

- [ ] Is it something I can "own" and become known for?
- [ ] Is it memorable?
- [ ] Does it set me apart from other artists?

Your niche doesn't have to be something that's never been done before; it just needs to have your special spin on it! A lot of this process will happen naturally, because, as we've explained before, you can't help but be yourself. However, it is very helpful to check out what other people are doing in a similar space in the market so you really understand where you can stand out. Remember, we're not here to copy or compare! You simply want to find what's missing that you can bring to the table.

> ***Before we move on, we also want to highlight that your work doesn't need to have profound meaning for it to be important or worthy of sharing.***

Your niche doesn't have to focus on something revolutionary and world-altering if that doesn't feel right to you. Your niche might just be your unique process. It might be based on your appreciation for nature or the type of clients you like to work with. It may be a particular mission or cause that drives all of your work. A niche can be any number of things. Whatever it is, creating your art at all is an act to be proud of and it's definitely worth sharing.

Your Artist Statement

Once you've found that nucleus, the heart-center that is your niche, it's SO important to make sure other people understand what it is, too! This is where your artist's statement comes in. We're going to help you craft a few sentences to describe your niche and your voice as an artist so that you can be sure you're communicating with clarity. Your statement will be your BFF when someone asks you the dreaded "What do you do?" question when you're stuck in an elevator together. It'll also be great for more practical applications, like adding to your website or sharing when you (fingers crossed!) get press opportunities. And, it'll keep you centered and focused—a reminder of the artist you want to be, and a helpful measuring stick to refer back to. Whenever a new opportunity arises or a question comes up about what direction you want to go next, checking back in with your artist statement can be a really helpful way to see if the choices you're making are aligned with the map you laid out for yourself.

There are a *lot* of ways to approach writing an artist statement, and the one that works best is the one that feels truest to you. That being said, here are some things we suggest your artist statement should do:

- [ ] Communicate succinctly (keep it to two or three sentences)
- [ ] Use the first person ("I" and "my")
- [ ] Paint a picture of what your art looks and feels like
- [ ] Define your niche and how you're different
- [ ] Give readers something to connect to (story)
- [ ] Reflect your personality and unique voice
- [ ] Avoid clichés or overused words that lack specificity (e.g., "whimsical," "playful," "pretty")

If you're thinking, "that's a lot of stuff to expect a two-to-three-sentence statement to do"—you're not wrong! To be completely transparent, crafting an artist statement is one of the most difficult parts of this process, and it'll take a bit of finagling before it feels exactly right. However, we have spent this entire book preparing for this very moment! You know all the ingredients that need to go into this pie, you've just gotta put 'em together and stick 'em in the oven. Let's take a look at some hypothetical examples of artist statements that we think work well.

1. A painter who depicts modern subjects in historical art styles

My paintings examine our generation's obsession with modern vices by exploring what they'd look like in different eras. By transporting the latest meme into a scene from the Renaissance, or placing a reality TV star at an idyllic Norman Rockwell–style dinner table, my work highlights the absurdity of the things we have come to value and encourages people (including myself) to question why they've become so important to us in the first place.

Why it works: This statement paints a very clear picture (pun intended) of this artist's work. It addresses all the threads of consistency that people can expect to see, from the medium (painting), to the style (varying historical styles), to the subject matter (modern vices). It also highlights the meaning behind the work, which draws people into the bigger story this artist is trying to tell.

2. A graphic designer who specializes in bold, vibrant brand designs

I'm a graphic designer who creates over-the-top brand identities that overflow with personality. I never shy away from color, I'm a great time at a party, and I'm always upping the ante. My clients understand that more is more, and they're ready for a brand makeover that absolutely no one will be able to ignore.

Why it works: This statement quickly identifies the artist's specialty and what you can expect from working with them (a vibrant, over-the-top brand identity). It does a great job conveying personality and setting the tone for who this artist is and what they value.

3. An illustrator who uses minimalist geometric shapes and limited color palettes

My work as an illustrator centers on minimalism and geometry, influences I picked up from the mid-century modern home I grew up in and fell in love with. Whether I'm making editorial graphics, creating a gig poster, or designing for apparel, I always enjoy finding creative ways to make the biggest impact with limited shapes, strokes, and color palettes.

Why it works: This statement shares some of this artist's story and background from the very beginning, which gives the reader a chance to understand and connect to them. It then lays out the hallmarks of the artist's illustration style and gives an idea of the range of work they create.

WANT MORE EXAMPLES?

Revisit the artist statements in chapter 2 for William Morris (page 46), Katie (page 50), and Ilana (page 53).

IF • YOU • CAN'T

EXPLAIN • • • IT

SIMPLY

YOU • • • DON'T

UNDERSTAND IT

WELL • ENOUGH

ALBERT EINSTEIN

If you're feeling a little intimidated by these examples or like you don't have a handle on your statement just yet, don't panic! We really love the idea of, you guessed it, asking for help! You can work with a friend (even if your friend is the internet) if you're feeling a bit tongue-tied. Also, remember this statement isn't set in stone. The way you write it today is a reflection of where you are *right now.*

> ***You're going to evolve, and when you do, you'll revisit this statement and change it to reflect who you've become.***

Take a deep breath, feel free to leave and come back if you need a break, and keep our tips and pep talks in mind. When you're ready, it's time to finally write your very own artist statement!

WRITE YOUR ARTIST STATEMENT

Use your word bank from page 93 and the examples we've provided previously to write your artist statement.

DRAFT

✱ FINAL ARTIST STATEMENT

THE ENEMY OF FEAR IS CREATIVITY

Seth Godin

Heck to the yeah! We obviously don't know what you wrote, but we'd love to hear it (check out Resources on page 173 for a free template so you can share it on social). We know how hard you've been working, and we feel like your two proud art moms who just wanna give you a big fat hug and stick everything you've ever made up on our fridge!

For the introverts who may have been sweating through their entire outfit while reading this chapter, we didn't forget about you! We know that talking about yourself and your work might be your actual worst nightmare, right up there next to public speaking in your underwear. We see you! And even if you aren't feeling like you're about to hurl, you're probably having at least some kind of self-doubt as you're working through this book, because, well, you're human. So, let's talk about it! A good place to focus is probably on one of the biggest sources of self-doubt there is—our unwanted but persistent companion: imposter syndrome.

ESSAY: Let's Talk About Imposter Syndrome

If you've ever felt like you're just making it up as you go, out of your league, beyond your depth, and likely to be outed as a total fake at any moment—congrats! You've met our dear friend imposter syndrome.

Yep, that's right—we know her, too, and we know her *well*.

We're actually hanging out with imposter syndrome right this very moment, as we're writing this book. We definitely didn't invite her to the party, but when she heard we'd gotten a book deal, she took it as an invitation to try to burst our bubble. She asks us all sorts of rude questions, like . . . "Who are YOU to think you're experts on this subject? What do YOU know?"

It's important to be honest with you about the fact that we're having these thoughts, because one of the biggest misconceptions about imposter syndrome is that it goes away after a certain milestone or level of "success." We tend to think, *When I land that dream client, it'll go away*, or *When I make a certain amount of money, it'll go away*, or *When I get a book deal, it'll go away*. But what we now know from personal experience, and from friends and family with plenty more life experiences than us, is that it doesn't. That sounds scary, but please don't despair; while it may never get the hint that you don't want it hanging around, you *will* get better and better at dealing with it as time goes on.

Think of imposter syndrome as your awkward cousin who always tries to bring up their weird conspiracy theories at Thanksgiving. They're always sharing news they got from a chain email as if it's fact, and you can't help but end up yelling at each other over the mashed potatoes by the end of the night. But, as you get older and have more uncomfortable family gatherings under your belt, you begin to realize that it's better to just pass the darn potatoes and do your best to not engage.

While "not engaging" with imposter syndrome may be a great strategy, we've got to be real with you—getting to that point takes a lot of discipline. And as artists and creatives, that's some of the deep soul work we're *always* going to have to do. It's a wave we'll continue riding, but we'll get stronger every time we do.

Being an artist is an innately vulnerable act. We're constantly taking risks by making things that no one has made before. *What if people don't like what we create? What if they look at our work and reject it?* We're always putting bits of ourselves into the world to be judged, and that is a very scary thing to do. When we start to turn our art practice into a business, we're inviting even *more* opportunities for imposter syndrome to creep in. Every time you put a piece of art up for sale or send your portfolio to a prospective client, you're suddenly asking them to put a literal value on something that you made from your heart. "How many dollars is this worth to you?" is a scary question to ask about a piece of art that feels like part of your identity. If they don't think your art is good enough—does that mean *you* aren't good enough?

N-O. We're going to go ahead and shut that one down *real quick*. You ARE good enough. These thoughts and feelings are 100 percent natural, but that does NOT mean that they are facts. You didn't just get lucky. You didn't barely scrape by. You aren't just keeping up with this facade that will come crashing down one day. You are not inadequate. You are not a fraud. Feel free to cut this out and duct-tape it to your forehead as needed.

Imposter syndrome brings up all sorts of limiting beliefs and feelings of unworthiness that are not actually founded in reality. It is the plague that kills so many creative voices before they can make enough work to start progressing toward their goals. It's the little devil on our shoulder telling us we're inadequate *despite* the evidence telling us otherwise.

The fact that you're here reading these pages means you're willing to face the hard stuff. You're fighting for yourself and the vision you have for your life, and for that, we applaud you. Learning to coexist with imposter syndrome takes a lot of practice, but we've got a few tips to help you find your way out of that glass case of emotion.

✱ Trust the facts, not the feelings. One important way you can combat imposter syndrome is by learning to trust *the facts* and *the proof* more than you trust *the feeling* of being an imposter. The next time you notice yourself leading with fear or anxiety, take a pause and ask yourself to list the facts. Almost every time, you'll discover that your emotions aren't based on truth or evidence, and they're actually keeping you from doing things that will ultimately benefit you.

A feelings-based thought might tell you, *I shouldn't go to that artist meetup because I've only been making art for a few months. I'm not a real artist, so I don't belong there.* A facts-based thought would say, *This meetup is for artists, which I am because I make art. I should go so I can meet other people in my community, and maybe I'll even find someone there who's more experienced than I am and can show me the ropes!* Using logic to evaluate the situation will often give you a boost of confidence and help quiet some of the fear that's holding you back.

I STILL BELIEVE THAT AT ANY TIME, THE NO-TALENT POLICE WILL COME AND ARREST ME.

MIKE MYERS

✱ Find your people.
The number-one thing that has helped us in our fight against imposter syndrome is finding a sense of *belonging*. When we feel like we don't fit in, we're not accepted, or we're not at the level of those around us, it makes us shrink. We get this feeling like we should get out of the way of the people around us, and the discomfort makes us tell ourselves stories about how others may perceive us that are almost always *not true*. This tends to happen most when a situation is new to us.

If we know that the feeling of belonging in a creative environment will help us thrive, the next step is to find (or build) that space or community. This may mean trying out different groups or going to different events related to your creative field until you find the right fit. Look for people who are in the same stage of their journey or career as you. Consider going to conferences or retreats. Check out your local creative meetups. Reach out to folks on social media (remember—we're only where we are today because of an Instagram DM!). If this type of thing doesn't freak you out, make it a point to be the person who finds the other people who are sitting alone (Ilana does this at events!). Nothing helps alleviate the sting of imposter syndrome more than finding your place with other folks who are going through the same things you are!

✱ No one knows what they're doing.
Another thing you can do to fight against those scary feelings of inadequacy is to understand how *incredibly common* it is to experience those emotions. While the concept of imposter syndrome was only first introduced in 1978 (originally called "imposter phenomenon"), the feeling has been around for ages. When you're face-to-face with self-doubt, remind yourself that all your favorite creators have had those same, nasty thoughts. Your favorite musicians, authors, designers, chefs—they've *all* looked at their creations and thought, *This is crap.* They've all wondered if they should just throw in the towel before someone discovers that they're not actually qualified to be doing what they're doing. But thank *goodness* they didn't let imposter syndrome win, right? What would the world be lacking if they listened to their intrusive thoughts and didn't make their art? The same goes for you. What magic might we all miss out on if you don't put your creativity to use? What joy and opportunities for growth would *you* not get to experience?

Truthfully, most of us are making it up as we go every single day. If you're waiting for the moment when you suddenly feel completely comfortable and assured in yourself or when you finally know all the answers, you're going to be sorely disappointed. We're so sorry to break it to you, but that's not a thing! No one actually feels like they've got it all figured out. But don't panic! If we understand that there's no ultimate moment where we'll finally banish imposter syndrome once and for all, we can actually *relax*. Discomfort is a sign of growth, because it means you're taking action that is pushing you outside the bubble of what your brain thinks is "safe." You're expanding your mind! You're opening yourself up. You're learning. And the more we take those risks and fight through the discomfort, the easier it becomes to do the things we don't feel equipped to do.

✳ We hold ourselves to impossible standards.

Many of us struggle with feeling like we're never good enough because we set completely unrealistic expectations for ourselves. Our brains tell us we've got to be the best—to do it all perfectly—or else we're a total fraud. *I can't call myself an artist until my paintings sell for thousands. I'm not a real designer because I didn't get a college degree like all my coworkers did.* We would never hold other people, especially our friends, to those expectations, so why are we so darn harsh with ourselves? Still, we constantly set higher goals the minute we meet the previous ones. It doesn't matter how much success or evidence we have telling us we're "enough," because we're much more prone to believe our negative thoughts than the positive ones (how uncool is that?).

It's difficult to change patterns of thinking, but we *can* do it. Katie has made major strides in the past few years learning to become more lenient and kinder to herself through talk therapy and intentional practice. Understanding the root of *why* you push yourself so hard can be vital to unlearning that behavior. When Katie dug into her own motivators, she discovered that she was relying on achievements and accolades to prove her worth to others while neglecting her own well-being in the process. Once you can put your finger on the core issue, it's much easier to catch yourself and reevaluate your thought process next time you fall into those same unhealthy behaviors.

We tell ourselves stories that ultimately become our reality, so start telling yourself a story that you'd actually like to see come true. Sure, imposter syndrome will always try to claw its way back in, but it won't be able to fully take hold if you're bringing the main character energy and calling the shots! Whether you prefer to meditate, manifest, journal, or something else entirely, the more you focus on the thoughts you *want* to think, the more they'll begin to actually take root and become your truth.

We know it's difficult, but you're exactly where you need to be, and you're taking steps in the right direction right this very moment. We're on your team, and we're cheering you on!

FROM KATIE

I've always felt completely out of place in any kind of sporty situation.

My "sports" growing up were theater and competitive roller skating, if that paints the picture for you (and much of my time at skating practice was spent on the sidelines, drawing in my calligraphy book). That made things really difficult in my adulthood when I realized I needed to start going to the gym to stay healthy. It was not a place that made me feel good, and whenever I walked into that environment, I immediately felt like all eyes were on me. In my head, everyone could see I didn't belong there.

However, I knew I had to actually make a change, and because the way I'd been approaching exercise previously hadn't worked, I needed to do something differently. I began searching for gyms and eventually stumbled on one that only offered group classes. When I'd felt alone and totally out of my depth before, I'd failed. Maybe if I had some support from other people, it would be different. Another thing that was even more important to me was that this gym was extremely beginner friendly. I saw pictures on their website of grandmas lifting weights (heck yeah!) and I saw people who looked like me—lots of them! That seemed like it could be a gym environment where I wouldn't feel so out of place, so my husband and I signed up.

If only past me could see the current me . . . her jaw would drop! Now I'm a regular gym-goer, doing deadlifts, bench presses, and back squats—all words that were completely foreign to me before. My mindset has totally transformed, and I honestly can't picture my future without exercise as a regular fixture because it makes me feel so good. This is one of the biggest transformations I've ever seen myself go through, and it's all because the instructors and members made me feel supported and welcomed—like I truly belonged in that space.

UNCOVERING LIMITING BELIEFS

Let's use this opportunity to do some unpacking. Below you'll find a list of questions to help you work through your own negative beliefs and fears related to imposter syndrome. If it helps, grab a friend, a cup of tea, and consider this your very own therapy session.

When do you think someone is allowed to call themselves an artist?

....

....

....

....

....

....

....

What do you think others expect of you when you tell them you're an artist?

....

....

....

....

....

....

What do you think a "successful" artist looks like? Are there certain achievements, metrics, or milestones that need to be met?

What are some achievements you've accomplished throughout your creative journey? Write them down even if they seem "small" to you.

When do you feel most like an imposter? Why do you think that is? If you were *actually unqualified* to be doing what you're doing... *what's the worst that could happen?*

AFFIRMATIONS

Now that your limiting beliefs are out in the open, you can start using the tools we've laid out in this chapter to help you dismantle them. A great first step is to begin incorporating affirmations into your daily routine to combat the false and negative thoughts that come up. Our internal dialogue becomes our truth, so the more we repeat the positive thoughts that we *want* to believe about ourselves, the more they'll begin to feel real.

Use the affirmations below or create your own, and schedule moments into your day to recite them to yourself. You can say the words out loud or in your head, but either way, try your best to actually believe them. It may feel inauthentic or uncomfortable at first, but the more you say them, the more honest they will become.

USE OUR AFFIRMATIONS or WRITE YOUR OWN

- I am not too much or too little.
- I am not too young or too old.
- I am good enough.
- I am unique and full of incredible ideas.
- My creativity will never dry up.
- I am allowed to be here.
- I deserve to be here.
- I deserve to do what makes me happy.
- I don't need anyone's validation but my own.

....

....

....

....

....

....

....

....

....

....

....

....

....

I DESERVE TO DO WHAT MAKES ME HAPPY

CHAPTER 6

Selling Yourself Without Selling Out

A note from your art moms:

If you're not planning to sell your artwork, take only what you need from this section. Approach this chapter with the knowledge that your artwork has impact, regardless of whether it has a price tag or not.

We've established that you do, in fact, need to share your work for people to find it. But how do you do that without immediately wanting to run in the opposite direction? How do you go about selling your artwork without losing yourself in the process?

The word "marketing" is kind of like the "Voldemort" of the art community: It's spoken about in hushed tones and is generally met with horror and revulsion when anyone dares to bring up the topic. We've heard from so many of our peers that they associate this word-that-shall-not-be-named with things like cheesy infomercials, email inboxes full of spam, and pop-up ads that just won't quit. Marketing has definitely gotten a reputation, and it's not a very good one.

> ***Despite all the baggage that comes with the topic, you don't actually have to sell your soul if you want to sell your art.***

There's a better way, folks, and it doesn't feel gross, and it doesn't require you to sacrifice all your morals. It's actually a pretty simple concept—one you're already very familiar with, because it's pretty much the theme of this whole book. That's right, the big secret of marketing is . . . (drumroll please) . . . *just be yourself.*

You've probably realized by now that showing up as your authentic self is the answer to a lot of the big questions that come with being an artist. You've been working hard to get in touch with your inner voice and figuring out what story you want to tell, so it would be pretty weird if we asked you to throw all that out the window when it comes time to actually share your art with the world. Really great marketing isn't about trickery or smoke and mirrors. It's all about honesty, real connections, and leaning into the unique qualities you've identified that set you apart.

Before we get into the specifics of how to create a marketing strategy that's founded in authenticity, we need to address some of the most common reasons that selling your art or creative services might give you the "ick." If you're anything like the hundreds of artists we've mentored in our courses and coaching sessions, you probably feel pretty uncomfortable having to "pitch" yourself or ask people for money. When we dig deeper into these feelings, we tend to find a few limiting beliefs lurking underneath, so let's take a moment to examine those.

Shifting Your Mindset

1. I'm an artist, not a businessperson—I don't have the skills for marketing.

Wanna know a not-so-secret secret? We didn't go to business school. But even without a business degree on our wall, we're still here, making our living by running our own businesses. The idea that you have to get a formal business education to be successful is outdated and untrue. And the misconception that creatives don't have the chops to handle business stuff is even more bonkers! Marketing, like most aspects of running a business, requires a *ton* of creativity. As an artist, you actually have a leg up, because you already use your creative problem-solving muscles all the time! Whether you're art directing product shots, writing captions, creating social media content, or designing your portfolio website, your creativity and your unique perspective should always be at the forefront of your marketing efforts.

Don't tell yourself you can't. You're more than qualified to tackle this!

2. I'm scared people will reject me.

Being yourself and sharing who you are with others is an act of vulnerability. It means you're taking a position, and some people won't like it. Some might even feel the need to tell you, even though you definitely didn't ask them. But you simply can't attract your true fans if you don't make room for the occasional "hater," too. Rejection never feels awesome, but we've learned to embrace it over the years. If our art or content repels certain types of people, that's a good sign that we're saying something of substance and making more room for the people who really "get it."

If you dim your shine and make yourself smaller, you might find people who like *you. But if you stand by who you are and let your voice ring out, you'll find the people who* love *you.*

3. I feel unworthy or guilty when I ask for money.

You have something *good* to offer—something that people want or need. You are helping people by sharing your work with them. Maybe you're bringing life to a blank space on their wall or helping their product sell because your gorgeous art is on it. Maybe you're bringing *their* brand voice to life and helping them express themselves with a logo. Those are all things that make someone's life better. You are *not* asking for a favor or a handout.

You deserve to make money from your art, and that does not change just because you enjoy what you do!

4. I don't want to be a "sellout."

If you're worried that commercializing your art will compromise your creative integrity, come back to authenticity—it's almost always the answer. Monetizing your art does mean you may occasionally make some different choices than you would if you were creating only for yourself, but it doesn't mean you have to sell your soul to the algorithm. You might just find that your customers respond to one product better than another so you decide to make more of that thing, or you might want to lean into one type of social media content because it performs best. But remember, there are no real rules around creating #content, despite what some "influencers" may tell you. The only rule, as far as we're concerned, is to follow your own arrow.

The direction you take and the way you interpret feedback is always your choice, and it should always be rooted in what feels right to you.

Marketing is ~~sleazy~~ storytelling.

The first step toward building a marketing strategy as an artist is to shift your mindset. When done well, marketing is just another avenue for personal creative expression and allows you to make deep, genuine connections with people who love what you do. Once you've laid that mental groundwork, we can start to build an actual marketing plan that details exactly what tactics you'll use to express your artistic identity to the world.

Finding Your People

One of the first things you need to do when defining a marketing strategy is to identify your ideal client (also known as your primary audience, target market, customer profile, etc.), so you can understand who you're speaking to. Other types of businesses often build their companies by starting with an audience first and *then* creating a product that serves the needs of that particular group. We've learned that artists thrive most when they do the opposite. As creatives, we almost always need to focus on self-discovery and identity FIRST, and THEN discover the audience that is attracted to that authentic self. If we aren't centered around making art that *we* love, it's really easy to end up feeling burned out and unfulfilled, and we definitely don't want that!

Since you've already done the work to uncover your niche, your artist statement, and the keywords that describe what makes you unique, it'll be a lot easier to figure out who your work attracts and who will benefit from it. Let's do that now.

DEFINE YOUR AUDIENCE

Take a few minutes to answer the following questions about your ideal audience—the people who want or need what you offer.

1. What are their defining personality traits and key values?

....
....
....
....
....

2. What problems or needs does your art solve for them?

....
....
....
....
....

3. Where do they spend their time (online and offline)?

....
....
....
....
....

4. What are their interests?

....
....
....
....
....

5. What is their age range and any other important demographics?

....
....
....
....
....

If you're a multi-passionate artist who offers several different products or services, you may be struggling a bit with this exercise. Maybe, like us, you work with freelance clients on one hand and educate artists on the other.

Or perhaps you paint murals but also license your art for greeting cards at the same time. If there are different parts of your business, you may end up having multiple audiences, and that's totally okay! You'll simply need to go through this exercise for each audience. Then, you'll also keep each audience in mind as we break down different strategies for marketing in the next section. As you decide which tactics you'll use to reach those groups, we highly recommend looking for places where your audiences overlap and focusing on those first. For example, if you're targeting both clients who want murals and clients who want to license greeting cards, you might concentrate on getting your work on Pinterest, because *both* types of clients will probably be looking for you there! If you're feeling overwhelmed as you begin to delve into a marketing plan for multiple audiences, that might be a sign to remove something from your plate, or to prioritize one part of your business over another until you find your rhythm.

Once you've identified your audience (or audiences), one really helpful way to get to know them better is by gently and politely stalking them. Don't worry, it's not as creepy as it sounds! Start by finding your ideal customers on the internet—whether it's on social media, a Reddit thread, or in the comments on YouTube. If you paint pet portraits and your audience is dog and cat owners, you could find forums or groups about pet ownership. Or, if you're a calligrapher who specializes in wedding invitations, you might check out some popular social accounts for wedding planning. Once you find your people, see what they're talking about—*especially* what they're complaining about.

> ***Knowing what your audience is saying and where their pain points are is so valuable, because then you can solve those problems and address those needs even better.***

Maybe you'll learn that people feel intimidated when hiring a wedding calligrapher because they don't know how the process works, and they feel silly asking. If you know that, you can make sure the messaging you use in your marketing approach breaks down what working with you looks like, step by step. You can focus on approachability and create a safe space for clients who have questions. Remember, the goal is never to change the core of what you do and who you are to appease someone else—it's simply to learn how to better communicate and meet your audience where they are. That's marketing in a nutshell!

Your Brand Is More Than a Logo

The next step in communicating your artistic identity is to create your branding. An artist's "brand" is just another form of storytelling—what words, symbols, imagery, and colors do you use to communicate who you are and what you offer? Of course, your actual artwork will do a ton of the heavy lifting by setting the vibe and forming the foundation of your brand, but it doesn't end there. Extending those visuals into other assets that you'll need to promote yourself, from your website to your typefaces to your logo, will help you paint a more complete picture and act as a beacon to draw in your target audience.

One of the first things you'll need to do when building your brand is to choose a name. If we can give you any advice on this topic based on our own experience, it would be to let go of some of the stress you're probably feeling around finding the *perfect* business name. We put a lot of pressure on ourselves to find the "right" name for our business in the beginning, only to end up hating it and changing it after a year or two. We get questions from our students all the time about whether they should just use their own name, add something like "design" to the end of their name, or if they'd be better off coming up with something totally different. Our answer is—it's honestly not that deep. We've learned that the most important part of the naming process is to pick one and embrace it. Your audience will come along for the ride!

Once you've got your name, it's time to nail down your logo (the wordmark, symbol, or combination of both that identifies your brand). This can be a scary moment for an artist, because we really can be our own worst clients. Again, our advice would be to let some of that perfectionism and pressure go before you drive yourself absolutely crazy trying to create the "best" logo. Your logo can be a fun, small part of your brand, but it will not make or break you. Because we know how difficult it can be to design for ourselves, we decided to hire someone else to create the Goodtype logo (shout-out to the team at Hoodzpah Design), and it allowed us to let go of a lot of that responsibility. Whether you're able to ask for help or plan to tackle it on your own, remember . . . this process should be fun, so let it be!

After your name and logo, you'll want to define other elements of your branding, like the typefaces you'll use, your color palette, and any other imagery you want to incorporate. These assets can help strengthen your message, and as trained graphic designers, we're all about eye candy. But, we also recognize that sometimes we just need to get scrappy and put something out there. *Done* is better than *perfect*!

> ***It's also important to keep in mind that, just like your work evolves, the elements you use to represent your brand are allowed to change too.***

No one expects you to remain stagnant, and no one's going to flip out if you decide to tweak your logo somewhere down the line. As you develop your brand, try to center yourself in the joy of it—you've discovered who you are, as a person and an artist, and now you get to express it!

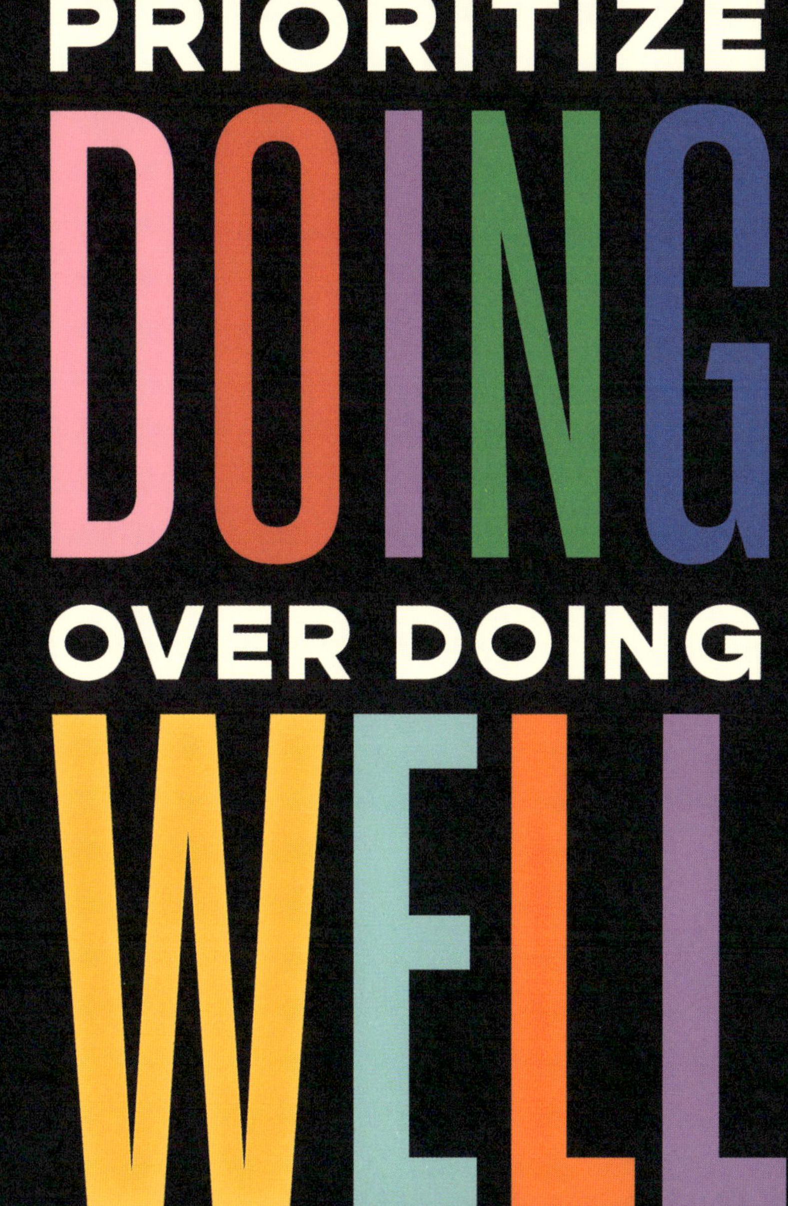
PRIORITIZE
DOING
OVER DOING
WELL

Your Website

Having a website is very important for artists these days, especially because it's one of the few platforms you have full control over. While social media apps can be great marketing tools, they are run by third parties that control who (and who doesn't) see your content. They are also free to make changes to their platforms or even totally disappear without notice. Your website is *your* domain, where you get to call the shots and showcase your work exactly as you like.

We tend to view our websites as the hub of our online presence—the epicenter that all our other channels and platforms ultimately lead back to. We use lots of tools to find our audience and connect to them, but when they're getting closer to making a purchase decision (buying a piece of art, hiring us for a freelance gig, etc.), we want them on our website, because that's where we can answer all their final questions and turn their "maybe" into a "yes."

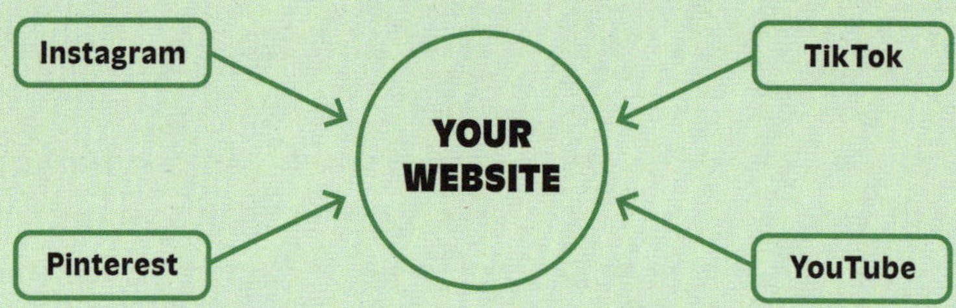

Your website should showcase your work, explain what you do and what you offer, and give people a clear way to get in touch with you. Even though the list of things your site should do is relatively short, creatives really like to overthink this piece of the marketing puzzle. We tend to want to overdesign our websites, and it can feel like a huge undertaking just to get started (which is why so many of us freeze before we ever begin). The truth is, if you're this deep in this book, *you're already at least 80 percent finished with your website.* Your site is really just a container, meant to hold all the things you've already busted your butt to create.

> ***Your artwork, your artist statement, your branding—those are the pieces that are doing the heavy lifting.***

If you're a web designer who's super passionate about making an interactive portfolio site with lots of bells and whistles to show off your web skills, we can totally see how you might want to go all out. But in most circumstances, we'd suggest letting your artwork do most of the talking, and keeping the web design simple and in more of a supporting role.

As you're building your website, make sure you spell out what kind of work you do and what you offer, and make it impossible to miss. Potential clients and customers need to be able to understand what they can hire you for or buy from you within ten to fifteen seconds of landing on your site. Like we mentioned before, you've already done this work. Start by incorporating language from the artist statement you wrote in the previous chapter, as well as the additional keywords you identified in chapter 4 (Reflecting & Putting the Pieces Together; see pages 92–93). You might want to place your artist statement at the top of your home page, right next to your art. Or maybe you pull out a piece of your statement for the home page and then fit the rest on the "about" page. The goal here is to quickly and concisely convey who you are so your audience gets hooked and excited to learn more!

When you're deciding what pieces of your work to include, you'll need to put on your curator hat. We're gonna get a little ruthless and make some tough cuts, *Project Runway* style ("Auf wiedersehen," baby!). We know how hard it is to be selective when it comes to your portfolio, especially when you're newer to the art world and don't have a huge body of work just yet, but curating helps you put your best foot forward.

It's good practice to leave out any kind of work that you don't want more of. In other words—don't want to design any more brochures? Cool! Don't put them in your portfolio, then. It's also helpful to dump anything that doesn't really feel like *you* anymore, or that doesn't feel as refined as your other pieces. We've both been art directors who have been in charge of hiring artists for various jobs, and even if we really like someone's work, just one project that feels out of place can be a big red flag. It's like Katie's college professor once told her: your portfolio is only as good as your weakest piece! Try to step into a potential client's shoes and ask yourself what would make you want to hire . . . *you*.

Don't forget to give whoever lands on your website a clear path to get in touch with you or make a purchase. You can (and should) *literally tell them* what you want them to do. We refer to this as a "call to action" or "CTA" in marketing lingo. You might include buttons throughout your site that say, "work with me," and link to a form where they can enter their information. Or, maybe, you guide people to your product shop to make a purchase. Whatever your end goal is, make it super obvious and encourage people to do that thing!

A strong brand identity and a solid website are a great start, but building an online presence and marketing your work is anything but passive. Now it's time to really show up as you choose the platforms you'll focus on and start connecting to your audience.

We know what you're thinking: *Which app is best? How many times a day should I post? How do I tame the beast that is "the algorithm"?*

There are a lot of questions that come up when you open the social media Pandora's box, but you actually already have everything you need to find your answers. All you have to do is use your audience as your guide. If you want to know where to invest your time, simply find out where they invest theirs! Which platforms are they using most, and how do they like to engage? If you're unsure what type of content will resonate, imagine it through the lens of your audience, and then test it with them. Adjust it and try something else when it doesn't perform well. You can also literally reach out and ask people questions if you want direct feedback. We've often had one-on-one calls with students or sent out surveys to eliminate the guesswork in figuring out what our community wants! But don't forget to factor yourself and your own preferences in, too. If you're not interested in offering what your audience is asking for . . . *don't do it.*

To protect your mental health and avoid burnout, we suggest picking just one or two of the top social platforms that your audience is using and that you actually enjoy keeping up with. Once you're on the platform(s) of your choice, it's finally time to start telling your story and connecting with your audience! That means sharing your work, expressing your personality and what's important to you, helping your audience with pain points or needs they may have, and letting your niche flag fly!

> ***Imagine that each post and decision you make is like setting out breadcrumbs so your people can find you.***

Before we get too deep into this topic, let's do a quick huddle and secret handshake to remember that social media is highly curated. As you build your social presence and spend time on whatever app you've chosen, you might be tempted to forget that fact, finding yourself in the doom-spiral that is imposter syndrome. If this happens, no sweat, just head back to pages 118–122 for a refresher on the tools you can use to crawl out of the ol' imposter hole. Do your best to remember that you deserve to take up space, wherever you are in your journey as an artist. Don't let fear keep you from sharing your art—people want to see it, and they want to know you!

And if your perfectionist side tries to rear its head, remember that the lifespan of a social media post is *very short,* so while we want to encourage you to be intentional, you don't need to put everything you do on a museum-worthy pedestal.

As you're developing your social presence, keep in mind that you don't need a large following to be successful. It might sound strange coming from the owners of an account with more than a million followers, but trust us—engagement, or how people interact with your content, is a much more important metric. A loyal fan base of one hundred people can be much more impactful than ten thousand people who aren't participating. Focus on building deep relationships with your true fans, and your business will thrive!

When you're ready to start creating content, we've got a few tips to help. First, we've found that breaking up our content into four or five category "buckets" keeps us organized and focused while still allowing room for fun and experimentation. Depending on the kind of art you make and the audience you're speaking to, you could have buckets like "short educational videos," "favorite sources of inspiration," or "process and behind the scenes." Once you've defined those categories based on what you want to create and what your audience wants to see, you'll create content that falls into each segment. This gives your feed a sense of consistency without too much restriction, while giving yourself a few guidelines to help generate ideas.

CREATE YOUR CONTENT BUCKETS

Think of a few categories you can use to organize your own social content.

✳ CATEGORY 1: ....

content examples

....

....

....

✳ CATEGORY 2: ....

content examples

....

....

....

✳ CATEGORY 3: ....

content examples

....

....

....

Most people struggle when it comes to how much and how often to post. The pressure to constantly create more and more content can feel overwhelming, so here are some things to keep in mind. First, you don't need to make something new every time you post. In fact, we highly discourage it. We're all about reduce, reuse, and recycle over here—squeezing as much juice as we can out of one piece of art. For example, you could post a static image of your art initially. Then, you could show a process video of how you created that same piece. Next, you could show it in several different color palettes and ask for people to vote for their favorite, or mock it up to see how it would look as a mural. That's four different posts right there . . . and we could keep going!

Whatever your content looks like, don't forget to make it easy for people to connect with you or buy your work. Include a call to action to tell your audience exactly what you want them to do when they see your post. Do you want them to comment and interact? Then ask them a question! Do you want them to head to your website and sign up for your email list? Tell them, and make it easy to do by including a link in your bio.

Don't you dare expect your social strategy to work overnight! When you feel good about what you've shared but don't see the stats you hoped for yet, splash yourself with some ice water and remember that you've gotta give it some time before you throw in the towel and pivot. If you're doing all these things—you've worked on your mindset—and you're *still* feeling a bit weird about selling your art through social media, it might be because you haven't found the right rhythm between active and passive selling yet. Active selling is when you post and say, "Hey, buy this thing!" Passive selling happens in between periods of active selling, when you're simply laying out those breadcrumbs and telling the story of who you are. A healthy marketing strategy incorporates both. Personally, we've found that roughly one active selling post for every ten passive posts feels pretty good to us and seems to work well for our audience, too.

This isn't some magic number or hard-and-fast rule, but we know our audience gets exhausted if we're constantly selling, and so do we!

> ***Overall, when you focus on building trust and connection first, you'll likely find that your customers are more excited to buy when you do have something to sell, and some of those uncomfortable feelings you may be having are bound to dissipate.***

Here's the big asterisk on all this stuff. We've said it before, and it bears repeating—you don't have to do everything all the time. Your mental health is most important, so when you need a break from social media, take one. If you're worried you're losing out on clients, focus on another marketing tactic that feels better for a while, like sending outreach emails instead. And speaking of . . . let's move out of the world of social media and into the topic of emails, shall we?

Email

There are lots of reasons why we love using email as a marketing tool. For one, it's a direct line of communication with your audience—you don't have to let an algorithm decide if it will show them your content or not. It's also a much more reliable channel than social media.

Our email list is our highest converting sales channel, and a lot of other business owners say the same thing. "Conversion" is an important word in the marketing world; it refers to how many people in your audience move from the "potential client" category to the "official client" category by making a purchase or hiring you for a service. Email marketing is really good at this for one simple reason—the people who sign up for your email list already like you! They wouldn't give you access to their precious inbox if they weren't interested in what you do. Because people on your email list are voluntarily opting in to hear directly from you, you'll find your most active and loyal fans there. But don't forget, even loyal fans need a balance of passive and active selling, so make sure to vary the content you're serving to your list.

Email marketing can be powerful, but the way you use it will vary depending on your audience(s) and the type of work that you sell. For instance, if you're selling original art or items in a shop, you'll want to build and nurture a list of fans and alert them whenever you drop a new product or have a sale. On the other hand, artists who primarily do freelance work would be better served by sending individualized outreach emails to potential clients to pitch themselves for projects.

We've seen many an artist shiver when they hear the word "outreach," but it's really not as scary as it sounds, and it has been THE most important tool we've used to grow our freelance practices. Outreach means approaching potential clients who fit within the audience profile you defined and offering your services to them, and while it may seem intimidating, it's actually pretty simple. All you need to do is identify the people who could benefit from your offerings and send them a quick introductory message! If you're a muralist, you'll find businesses you think could benefit from a mural. If you're a brand designer, you'll find companies that could use a brand refresh or new companies that are just starting in your ideal market space. Then, you just craft an email that introduces yourself and shows a selection of your work, tell them how you can help them, and ask for a follow-up or give them a call to action of some kind.

It's common to feel a bit uncomfortable when you first begin an outreach strategy. Cold emailing means opening yourself up to the possibility of rejection, and as we've discussed before, that's a vulnerable thing to do. However, we've sent hundreds if not thousands of outreach emails between the two of us, and honestly, people have very rarely been unkind in their responses. We've gotten plenty of unanswered emails, but we've never had anyone come back with "gross, I hate your work!" Outreach takes a bit of bravery and plenty of patience, but the opportunities we've found and the doors it has opened have been SO worth our time.

FROM ILANA

While it seems unlikely that a social media app will disappear randomly, it absolutely could.

We actually got a taste of this while writing this book! The night before our online conference for artists, The Kernference, our entire Instagram account disappeared and was blocked. I nearly peed my pants! While we absolutely had some moments of panic, we were also *so thankful* that we had built an email list. Even if we didn't get our Instagram back (which, thankfully, we did), we wouldn't have had to start building our audience back up from scratch. What a relief!

ASK FOR WHAT YOU WANT

Other Marketing Tactics

Let's take a quick tour of some of our favorite marketing opportunities that we haven't covered yet—but remember, the list doesn't end here. Any tactic that gets you in front of your target audience and feels good and authentic to you is worth exploring. The only limit is your own creativity!

Pinterest is one of our favorite marketing tools, especially for artists. While it has a few social media–esque components, it really works more like a search engine, which means your work has a longer lifespan and many chances to be discovered. When pinning your work on Pinterest, you'll want to use keywords that describe your content in the caption so that people can find it when they search. Then, link back to your website, where people can learn more about you and how to purchase from you. Many types of audiences are on Pinterest—from art directors looking for artists to hire to art enthusiasts looking for the right piece to hang on their wall. If your target market uses Pinterest, this could be a great place to invest some time.

Keywords are extremely important, even outside of Pinterest, when you're trying to get found on the internet. The strategic use of these words and phrases is called SEO, or search engine optimization, and they tell search engines like Google what your content is about. When you tag your content with the proper descriptors, it will then begin to show up in search results when people are looking for those keywords. There are *lots* of tips and tricks for improving your SEO on your website and other platforms—so many that there are whole books and courses dedicated to the subject! We obviously can't give you the full rundown on SEO right here, so we encourage you to seek out more information if this is a tactic you're interested in.

Paid advertising is another path to consider, but it's a bit more advanced. We don't typically suggest running paid ads when you're just starting your business, or before you have a product or service that seems to be selling well already. However, if one of your offerings is really popular, it might be a good idea to add fuel to a fire that's already burning bright!

Appearances and guest features on podcasts, YouTube channels, conferences, blog posts, etc. are a great way to establish your expertise and reach new people. We highly recommend pitching yourself for these opportunities using the outreach email strategies we talked about earlier. Plus, the more people who see you speaking, engaging with your community, and expressing yourself, the more likely they'll be to trust you and, ultimately, buy from you.

Many artists' success stories are shaped by the relationships they build and the people they meet throughout their career.

> ***Never underestimate the power of networking, and always make an effort to be kind to the people you encounter!***

One powerful relationship you may want to consider pursuing is with a mentor. When you find someone in your industry who's doing what you'd like to do, you can simply ask them if you can assist or shadow them. An aspiring muralist might help out on an install, a new photographer might volunteer as a second shooter, and a budding brand designer might act as a production assistant. Not only will you get to learn the ropes, but you'll put yourself in real, professional situations where you can start to create your own network. If you're able to find someone to be your mentor, just make sure to return the favor once you've found your place in the industry by helping new up-and-comers. Be cautious of other people's time, and know that a mentor has their own job and life to balance. A great way to get started is to offer to buy them a coffee and learn more about them. If you're not in the same location, you can definitely use your creativity to try to get a bit of their time virtually.

Another relationship-based marketing tactic we haven't mentioned yet is referrals. People trust a friend's opinion much more than a random Google search, which is why word-of-mouth recommendations are so powerful. To encourage referrals, you might offer incentives for clients who bring you new work—perhaps a percentage of the job you end up booking, or a discount on their next project with you. Another way to foster organic referrals is to make sure you're giving your customers an amazing experience when they work with you.

Your Marketing Plan

We've given you lots of marketing methods to think about, but it all means nothing if you don't put it into action. Let's decide on the strategies you want to use and create a marketing plan so you can actually start making moves!

When we're creating our own plan, we like to break the year into ninety-day sections or quarters. Looking at the year in smaller chunks makes everything feel less overwhelming.

So, considering only the next ninety days, begin by defining a goal that will give you a clear idea of what you're working toward within this period. The goal you pick will depend on where you are in your business and what your current needs are.

It may simply be to increase awareness and start building your audience. It could be to book more clients. Whatever your goal is, we want to make it as concrete as possible so that you can know *exactly* how you are progressing as you work to achieve it. To do that, you'll need to attach some sort of number to your goal. For example, instead of "increasing awareness," your goal could become "get one hundred new followers on [insert social media platform here]." The objective is still the same, but it's now much more specific, which makes it easier to plan for!

> ***You may give yourself multiple goals, but remember—the more you overload yourself, the more likely you are to not achieve any of your goals because you're spread too thin!***

After you've settled on your goal, it's time to define the most important actions you want to take to reach it. Think about the marketing tactics we just laid out and decide which ones would be most relevant to your goal and effective for your audience. If your objective is to get one hundred new followers on social media, how will you do that? Perhaps you could co-create a post with another creator who has an overlapping audience? Maybe you want to go to some IRL networking events and bring a QR code so people can easily follow your account after they meet you. Start brainstorming now, and then let's put pen to paper and map it out!

FROM ILANA

The goal we just described is a *quantitative* one—something you can measure with numbers. These goals are specific and measurable, which makes them essential for tracking progress.

But here's the thing: numbers alone don't tell the whole story. That's where *qualitative* goals come in. Qualitative goals focus on the *experience* or *emotional impact* of what you're trying to achieve. They're less about hitting a specific target and more about how the journey feels.

Here's how I like to approach it: I take my quantitative goal and unpack the *why* behind it—the emotion or value driving me—and create a "sister" goal to measure success qualitatively. That way, whether I hit the numbers or not, I can still reflect on questions like:

- **Did I feel fulfilled while doing this?**
- **Did I enjoy the process?**
- **Was I challenged in a meaningful way?**
- **Was it sustainable?**

By reflecting on both types of goals, you'll set yourself up for wins that feel truly aligned with your values. And here's the kicker: even if you don't hit the number-driven goal, there's a good chance you'll succeed on the qualitative side, which is just as powerful—sometimes even more so.

YOUR NINETY-DAY MARKETING PLAN

Define your goal, then choose five to eight actions that you'll do to achieve it.

✱ GOAL

....

....

....

....

....

....

✱ ACTIONS

1. ....
2. ....
3. ....
4. ....
5. ....
6. ....
7. ....
8. ....

Once your plan is complete, we recommend adding due dates to each task to keep yourself on track. Then . . . start putting your plan into action! If you find yourself struggling with time management or productivity, the *New York Times* bestselling book *The 12 Week Year*, by Brian P. Moran and Michael Lennington, is a great resource to help.

Phhhheeeewww. That chapter was a doozy, wasn't it? We're not going to lie—marketing is a BIG topic and can feel overwhelming, but it's so important if you want to make money as an artist. As much as we wish we could just create all day without ever worrying about any of this stuff, alas, the world doesn't seem to work that way. Thank goodness, though, that there are ways to make marketing fun!

> ***You don't have to be sleazy and manipulative to sell your art; you just have to be yourself.***

So, as we send you off into the world, little marketing butterflies, don't forget to enjoy the process, embrace connections, and listen to your gut.

You got this!

ESSAY: Work-Life Balance

Unfortunately, we feel extremely qualified to talk about the struggles of trying to find work-life balance because we've often worn far too many hats at once. We should probably add "professional jugglers" to our resumes. Ilana, whose ADHD is another master of distraction she has to combat, always has ten balls in the air, and Katie has struggled with chasing the highs of achievement-based praise and validation from others. (Shout-out to therapy and medication for helping us with these issues!) In real life, we can't actually juggle, but we've had to spend a lot of time in our adulthood unlearning and reprogramming our brains so that we can live healthier lives—and we're still working on this today! While our drive and ambition have led us to some exciting places in our careers, it's also important that we acknowledge the negative effects those qualities can have when left to their own devices.

Ilana wrote her first book, *Mind Your Business*, while also nursing a newborn and creating hundreds of pieces of art for her art-licensing agent. She was used to operating with too much on her plate, since she'd previously been working a full-time job only to come home and spend every night and weekend building her own art business, but it really hit differently when she suddenly had a baby in her arms. She had been doing what she thought she was "supposed" to do to grow a successful business, but instead, she found herself with a one-way ticket to exhaustion and burnout. Becoming a parent, even with an incredibly involved partner and family, really gave her a reality check and became her catalyst for change. When someone's *life* literally depended on her, all those emails in her inbox suddenly seemed much less urgent.

According to Katie, Ilana would still probably win the award for most likely to answer your email in a timely manner, but she's learned to give herself more time and grace than she used to.

For Katie, it was her body that gave her a big "hell no" after too many late nights and self-imposed deadlines. She'd just left her job as an art director to start her own art business and had completely overloaded herself with high expectations, which ended up sending her right into the emergency room with a panic attack. The onset of her panic disorder made Katie realize she had to make some big changes, and over many years, through therapy, medication, and lifestyle changes, she has thankfully made a lot of progress and adjusted her workload to be much more sustainable.

BALANCE IS NOT SOMETHING YOU FIND IT'S SOMETHING YOU CREATE

JANA KINGSFORD

THERE IS
NO SUCH
THING AS
AN ART
EMERGENCY

We're sharing these personal stories not to scare you, but to encourage you to take better care of yourself than we did in the beginning. We've agreed there's no real "art emergency" that can't wait a few days. Despite how our society operates, perfectionism isn't a badge of honor. Burnout isn't just par for the course. We've got to reset the way we think about this stuff and prioritize our mental and physical health. Life is a marathon, not a sprint, and if we want to make it to the finish line, we've gotta give ourselves a freakin' break every now and then. Turns out, there's no trophy at the finish line. In fact, it's not even a race at all, so there's no need to run full-speed.

We both experienced life-changing events that forced us to reevaluate our work-life balance (or lack thereof). We needed to Marie Kondo our lives, because everything we'd taken on simply didn't fit anymore. The question was no longer "What should I add to my plate?" but "What can I remove that is no longer serving me?" That simple question is actual *gold*. And while it came to us in a time of ultimate stress and burnout, hopefully it's coming to you now before you've hit the bottom of your own spinning circle of doom. Try asking yourself this question now, and let's see what you can cut out of your life to make more room for the good stuff!

Another perspective shift you can make is to stop seeing "work" and "life" as things that need to exist in perfect equilibrium. They're intertwined, because life is complex and fluid, and our lives are never going to be 50 percent work and 50 percent play. So perhaps let's stop looking for work-life "balance" and start searching for work-life "harmony" instead. Let's follow along with the ebbs and flows of life and make adjustments where we need to, as if we're riding the seesaw of life. A seesaw would be incredibly boring if both sides were equally weighted! No one wants to just sit in the middle, never getting to experience the highs and lows of being human.

Maybe your idea of work-life harmony means working extra hours for a few days so you can take a snowboarding trip later in the week. Maybe it's taking a personal day and taking yourself to the movies for no particular reason at all. Or it could be saying *no* to a project inquiry (gasp!). And of course, let's not forget that one of our biggest goals, and probably one of the reasons why you're reading this book, is to get to do work that feels like play. We don't want a job that we'll always desperately need a break from—we want a job doing something we love. Part of the work-life harmony we want to achieve comes from finding enjoyment in all aspects of life . . . *including* work. Congratulations—you're already on the right track with that one!

LETTING GO AND MAKING ROOM

Take inventory of the tasks that you do regularly—your hobbies, commitments, and relationships.

What do you dread the most?

Can you remove any of those tasks from your plate? Can you delegate them or ask for help?

What drains you, or brings your mood down?

How can you restructure your life so that you're prioritizing the things that make you feel *good*?

What gets in the way of the stuff you really enjoy?

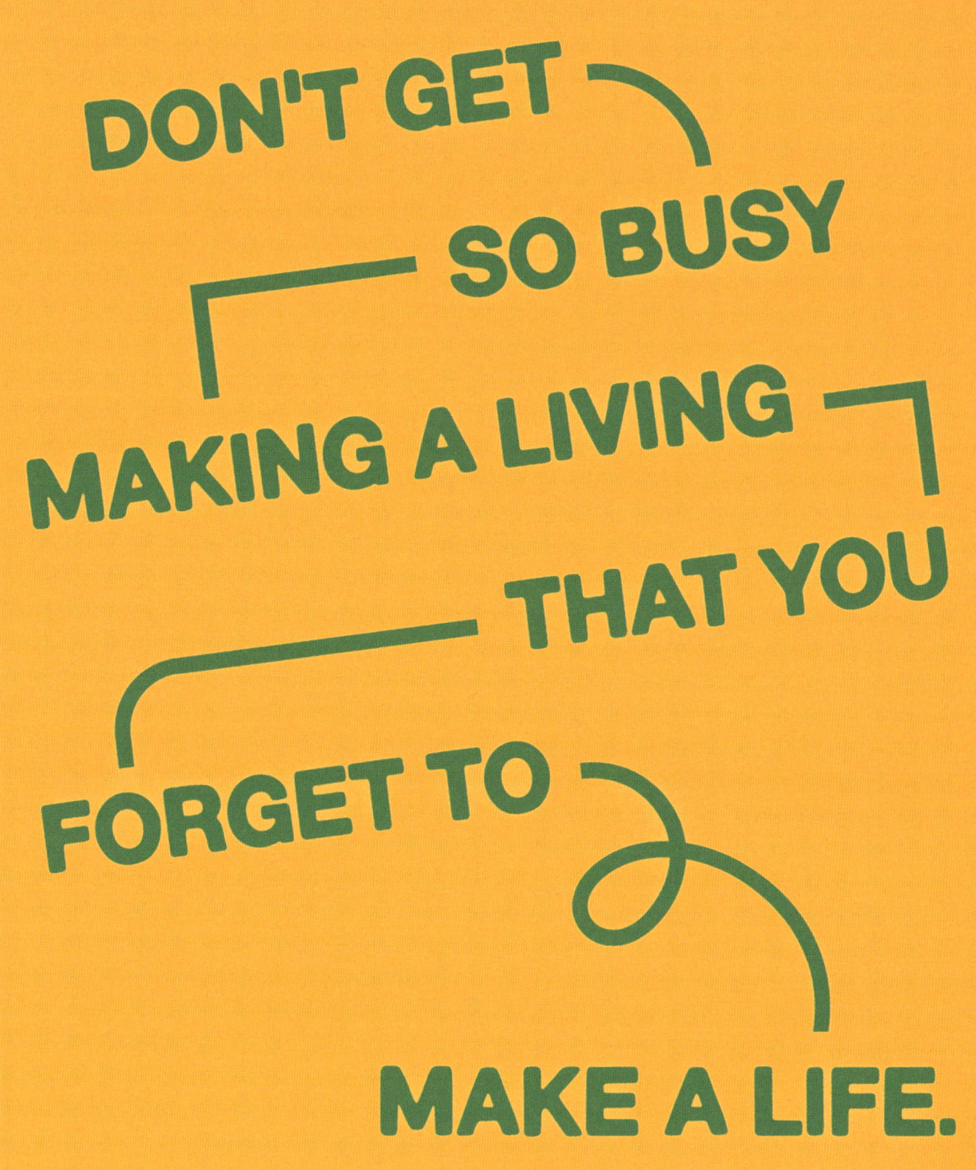
DON'T GET
SO BUSY
MAKING A LIVING
THAT YOU
FORGET TO
MAKE A LIFE.
DOLLY PARTON

MAKING MONEY FROM YOUR ART

Loving your job is truly a gift, but sometimes when we make a career out of what we love to do, we suck a bit of the magic right out of it. The best advice we have for artists in this position is to find opportunities outside of your work to stretch your creative muscles. From learning to knit to experimenting with makeup or DIY home decor—whatever it may be—find other ways to be creative and make a rule that you're *not* allowed to monetize them (we know it's tempting!).

FINDING TIME FOR PLAY

Brainstorm a few creative activities that you want to try just for fun. Then, when you find yourself in a rut or running low on inspiration, come back to this list and choose an activity!

✳ CREATIVE ACTIVITES

If you feel like you're stuck on the hamster wheel and have a difficult time removing tasks from your work plate, consider the productivity tools we're about to share with you. Figuring out what systems set you up to get things done more efficiently is a great way to inch toward a more harmonious life. While these are all strategies we've found helpful to us, it's important to remember that there's no "right" answer, and your only goal is to find what works for *you*.

1. Find your most productive working hours.

You might be a morning person like Ilana, but that doesn't necessarily mean that's your most productive time. You might love waking up and having a quiet morning reading a book and watching the sunrise (wait, this sounds so romantic!). Maybe you wake up to two screaming children who need your attention and it's not even an option to work in the morning. Perhaps you're useless before noon and need to shift your schedule later (Katie used to work better this way!). Document how you use your time for a week and see what times of day you feel the most inspired and the most productive. Then, schedule your working time on your calendar to align with those time blocks if you can. Consistency is important, but we all know that life *literally* happens, and some days it just won't be possible to work at your optimum times. Leave room for flexibility by giving yourself a buffer and be kind to yourself when life makes you go a little off script.

2. Find a dedicated "office" if you work from home.

It doesn't matter if it's just a specific chair or a pair of slippers—find a way to differentiate your environment so that you can more easily "clock in" and "out" of your office. This can be incredibly challenging for those who work from home, where pants aren't actually required and the call of the dirty dishes can be mighty distracting! For Ilana, getting dressed (even just changing into clean sweatpants) tells her brain that it's time to get to work. Katie's "office" is a comfy spot on her couch, and she makes sure to close her laptop when work is done for the day, so she's not tempted to just "hop on real quick" to answer an email at dinnertime!

3. Systematize and automate whatever you can.

Are there tasks you find yourself doing over and over? Let's think about how we can simplify, automate, and templatize those tasks whenever possible and save you some time and effort! Maybe you're constantly getting the same questions in your email inbox. What if you make some templated responses to the top five emails you get most often? Are you keeping your to-do lists scattered on sticky notes around your house? What if you use an online project management system to keep yourself organized instead? Ilana and Katie use Notion, a productivity and organization app, to keep tasks and reminders all in one spot.

CREATING SYSTEMS

Make a list of the tasks you do repetitively or the things that take up way too much time in your day.

✳ TASKS

1. ....

2. ....

3. ....

4. ....

5. ....

Pick one of the tasks above and answer the following questions (you can do this for each of them if you want).

What process do you currently use to complete this task?

....

....

....

....

....

....

....

How can you make the process more organized and efficient?

....

....

....

....

....

....

....

4. Prioritize your tasks.
When it feels like your to-do list is never-ending (truth bomb: it is), time management strategies help you reduce stress and increase productivity to get things done. The Eisenhower Matrix, which apparently isn't called "the urgent vs. important diagram," as we've thought for the past ten years, is a great place to start.

THE EISENHOWER MATRIX

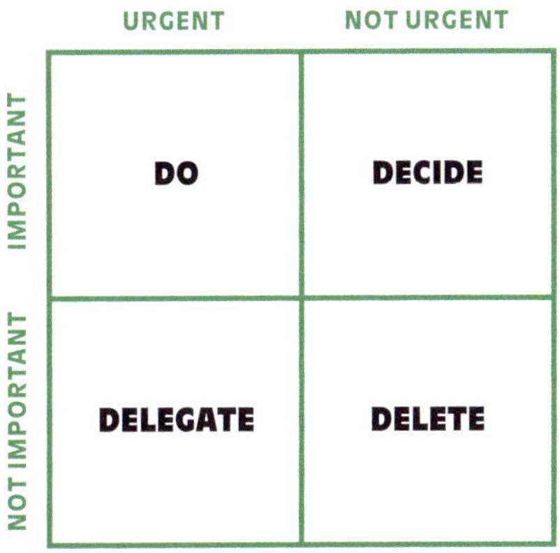

	URGENT	NOT URGENT
IMPORTANT	DO	DECIDE
NOT IMPORTANT	DELEGATE	DELETE

The Eisenhower Matrix is made up of four quadrants labeled "important" and "not important" on one side, and "urgent" and "not urgent" on the other. The first step is to figure out where each task on your to-do list lands on the matrix, based on its importance and urgency.

Once you've mapped out where your tasks belong, you can take the actions that correspond to the quadrant each task landed in. If your task is in the first quadrant (top left), it needs to be done first, because it's both urgent and important. These are your top priorities. The tasks in the second quadrant (top right) need to be decided on or scheduled. You don't need to take immediate action, but you do need to make a plan for completing them. For example, the laundry can be folded tomorrow. We like to put these items on the calendar, so we don't forget them. The third quadrant (bottom left) is not important but still urgent. Tasks like responding to generic email inquiries that you get all the time might go here. You can delegate these tasks to someone else or to an automated system, as we just discussed in the previous section. Finally, if your task falls into the final quadrant (bottom right), it's neither urgent nor important, meaning it might be time to cut ties and cross it off your list altogether.

TO-DO LIST

List the items on your to-do list for today, then practice using the Eisenhower Matrix to create a plan of attack. Circle one of the actions.

1. ....

....

Do Decide Delegate Delete

2. ....

....

Do Decide Delegate Delete

3. ....

....

Do Decide Delegate Delete

4. ....

....

Do Decide Delegate Delete

5. ....

....

Do Decide Delegate Delete

6. ....

....

Do Decide Delegate Delete

5. Don't forget to refill your cup. Ironically, making time to *not* work is one of the most productive things you can do. The more you push yourself to create when you're feeling uninspired or to work when you need to rest, the worse your performance will be. We all need to recharge, so build in time for that, too! (Like, literally put it on the calendar. It's just as important as the other stuff you have on your schedule!)

This whole book is about listening to yourself and building a life and an art practice that make YOU happy. The key word in all of this is YOU, so try your best to block out all the other noise, pressure, and preconceptions you may have about what work-life balance looks like to others, and focus on what *you* want it to be. If you could rebuild your life from the ground up, what would it look like? That life isn't just a daydream; it's the one you deserve. Now's the time to take stock of what's working and what you want to change, so you can take steps toward making your dream life a reality.

You deserve it, so go get it!

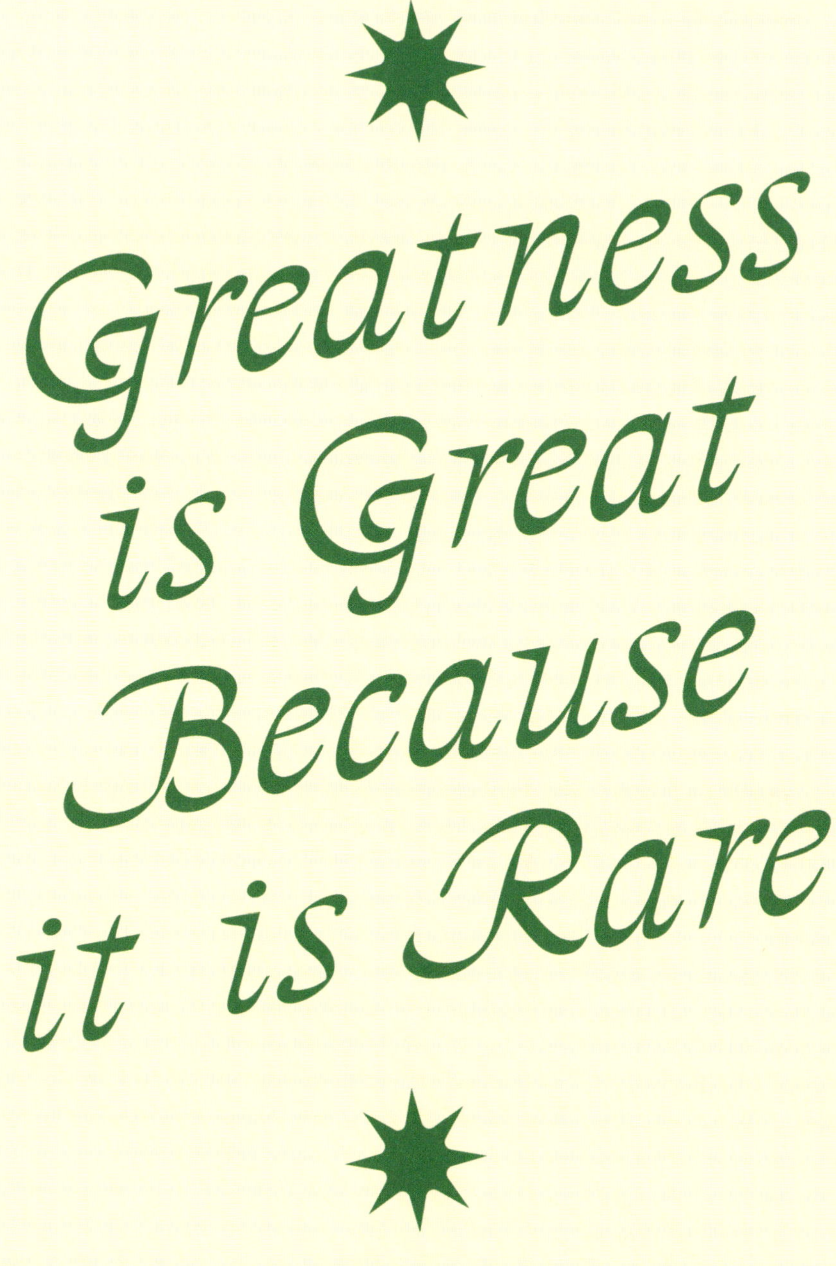
Greatness
is Great
Because
it is Rare

CONCLUSION

Pep Talk

Now that you've done the hard work to unearth your creative identity, congratulations, you're completely finished doing hard things for the rest of your life! *Just kidding.* You know us better than that by now. We couldn't let you go without giving you some homework—it just wouldn't feel right!

Your job moving forward is to keep the line of communication you've established with yourself *open*. Keep listening to your inner voice, and be your own observer. Remember, you're allowed (and encouraged) to change. The only thing we ask is that you try to stay mindful and in touch with yourself as you do. There *will* be outside influences and internal conflicts that challenge you, from imposter syndrome to creative block to difficult life circumstances, but hopefully this book will equip you with the tools to stay centered, even when it's really, really tough.

One of the challenges that you'll likely face on your creative journey is the temptation to become "the best." While competitiveness might seem harmless at first, it's easy to lose yourself and the identity you've worked so hard to uncover when you're busy trying to one-up everyone else. If you're looking for true fulfillment, you're much more likely to find it when you're coming from a place of authenticity instead of fighting for the top spot on a podium. Being a creative isn't about being the greatest, it's about figuring out your own mission and finding ways to share it so that others can connect with it, too. Even Enrique Olvera, the world-famous mole chef we introduced in the beginning of this book, has said, "We are not trying to make the best mole, just our own."

One of the most helpful things you can do to stay grounded in your authentic self is to surround yourself with other people who support and love you for who you are. Whether it's a family member, friend, or group of internet buddies, find the folks who really let you be yourself, and keep 'em close. We really found "our people" on social media when we began to participate in lettering challenges and started finding our footing in the online typography community. If you're still searching for *your* people, there are lots of places to look! You might try attending some local meetups for people that share some of your interests or messaging someone who interests you on social media. Our Goodtype community is also a great place to start! All are welcome, and we've included lots of ways to get involved in Resources (opposite). Putting yourself out there is hard, but finding the people who really get you is the greatest reward.

Whenever you find yourself face-to-face with doubt, fear, or creative block, try to remember that you are not alone, and that these are issues we all grapple with. Then, go back to the "recipe" you discovered for your own creativity in this book. Remember your why, revisit the components and characteristics that make you and your art unique, and start creating using those qualities as your foundation. It may help to view your recipe as your own set of "rules" that will help you find consistency and clarity whenever you embark on something creative. The beauty of these "rules" is that since you're the one making them, you also get to decide when to break them. Having a flexible formula to start from allows you to create with less pressure and judgment, and it gives you the confidence to get started when you're having a hard time deciding where to begin.

Props to you, one last time, for being here and valuing your own happiness enough to work for it. Your art deserves to be seen, shared, loved, and paid for, and you're taking all the right steps to get to where you want to go. Keep exploring, and invite possibility into your life as you continue to evolve and understand your own identity. You already have all the tools, inspiration, and know-how.

Now it's time to create.

RESOURCES

We've compiled all the resources we mention throughout the book onto a webpage:

GOODTYPE.US/FYA-RESOURCES

THE

PRIVILEGE

of a

LIFETIME

is to become

WHO YOU

REALLY ARE

CARL GUSTAV JUNG

ACKNOWLEDGMENTS

Lots of love to:

- Our families, for supporting us through every deadline and politely nodding through our super niche design rants.

- Our publishing team, for helping us bring the best version of this book to life.

- The Goodtype community, for constantly inspiring us to remember our "why."

- Each other, for being partners in type crimes, creative chaos, and all the challenges and joys that shaped this book. We're better together.

And to the readers and artists who keep showing up: May this book remind you that learning to be yourself is the most meaningful work you'll ever do.

ABOUT THE AUTHORS

Katie Johnson and **Ilana Griffo** are artists, authors, and the creative duo behind Goodtype—a vibrant community of over one million designers who love typography.

Through Goodtype, they provide education, resources, and inspiration to help other artists thrive doing what they love. They also create collaborative artwork through Goodtype Studio, with past clients including Target, Trader Joe's, Amazon Music, Adobe, Penguin Random House, and more.

Ilana Griffo lives in Rochester, New York, with her bike-racing husband, Gregg, and their two kids. She thrives on bringing order to chaos—a superpower that shows up just as much in her management of Goodtype's inbox as it does in her geometric, pattern-filled illustration work. Her first book, *Mind Your Business*, is an Amazon bestseller and has been featured in *Forbes*, Buzzfeed, and more. She's also a big fan of dogs and chocolate, though not at the same time.

Katie Johnson is a hand-lettering artist based in Austin, Texas, where she lives with her musically gifted husband, two cats, and a very beloved Aussiedoodle. Her love of ornament, filigree, and meticulous detail makes her the unofficial manager of minutiae at Goodtype. Though she spent her early years roller skating competitively and performing in every musical she could, these days you're more likely to find her writing songs, bingeing reality TV, or getting lost in an endless queue of fantasy and sci-fi audiobooks.